JAMES HOGG

MEMOIR OF THE AUTHOR'S LIFE

FAMILIAR ANECDOTES OF SIR WALTER SCOTT

JAMES HOGG

Memoir of the Author's Life

and

Familiar Anecdotes of Sir Walter Scott

EDITED BY

DOUGLAS S. MACK

University of Stirling

1972
SCOTTISH ACADEMIC PRESS
EDINBURGH & LONDON

Published by
Scottish Academic Press Ltd
25 Perth Street, Edinburgh 3
and distributed bv
Chatto & Windus Ltd
40 William IV Street
London W.C.2

ISBN 07011 1846 6

Printed by R & R Clark Ltd, Edinburgh

CONTENTS

Preface   vi
Introduction   vii

Memoir of the Author's Life   1
Commentary   82
Familiar Anecdotes of Sir Walter Scott   93
Commentary   136

PREFACE

THE two works reprinted here are well known as sources for the study of Scott and his period, and both have been frequently quoted by scholars. Unfortunately, however, they are seldom read in their entirety, mainly because complete texts have been difficult to obtain. The main object of the present edition is to make readily available reliable texts of Hogg's entertaining and informative memoirs.

No book of this kind could be prepared without the services provided by librarians, and I am particularly grateful to my former colleagues in the National Library of Scotland and in St Andrews University Library, and to my present colleagues in Stirling University Library. My thanks are also due to the Pierpoint Morgan Library, New York, for permission to reprint the *Familiar Anecdotes* from Hogg's manuscript, now in that library; and to the Trustees of the National Library of Scotland for permission to quote from the Hogg manuscripts there.

This book was read in typescript by Dr W. R. Aitken of the University of Strathclyde's Department of Librarianship, and I would like to record my especial gratitude to him for his most helpful criticisms and advice. I have also received valuable help from A. Bell of the National Library of Scotland, and from J. Kidd and R. N. Smart of St Andrews University Library. In addition, I would like to thank Dr J. C. Corson, who very kindly provided me with information and answered various questions for me. Errors and faulty judgements in the book are of course entirely my own.

Finally, I would like to thank my wife for all the help she has given me in the preparation of this volume.

Douglas S. Mack

University of Stirling

INTRODUCTION

JAMES HOGG was born in 1770 in the parish of Ettrick, which in 1792 was described as follows by its minister in the first *Statistical Account of Scotland:*

> This parish possesses no advantage. The nearest market town is 15 miles distant. The roads to all of them are almost impassable. The only road that looks like a turnpike is to Selkirk; but even it in many places is so deep, as greatly to obstruct travelling. The distance is about 16 miles, and it requires four hours to ride it. The snow also, at times, is a great inconvenience; often for many months, we can have no intercourse with mankind. It often also obliges the farmers to fly with their flocks to Annandale for provision. Another great disadvantage is the want of bridges. For many hours the traveller is obstructed on his journey, when the waters are swelled. . . . In this parish there are 12 ploughs, and 20 carts, but no carriages.

The whole of Hogg's childhood was spent in this remote and isolated community.

When he was six years old his father, a tenant-farmer, became bankrupt. It was necessary for the young Hogg to leave school, which he attended for only a few months in all, and the rest of his childhood was spent in service on various farms. Hogg later said that between the ages of six and fifteen "I neither read nor wrote; nor had I access to any book save the Bible".

Naturally enough when he did try to write again in his late teens he experienced considerable difficulty: "I was about this time obliged to write a letter to my elder brother, and, having never drawn a pen for such a number of years, I had actually forgotten how to make sundry letters of the alphabet; these I had either to print, or to patch up the words in the best way I could without them." In spite of these formidable disadvantages the first publication of Hogg's distinguished literary career—a poem contributed anonymously to the *Scots Magazine*—appeared when he was only twenty-three.[1]

In 1813 when he was forty-two years old Hogg's long poem *The Queen's Wake* was published. This work immediately made him a

---

[1] "The Mistakes of a Night", *Scots Magazine*, vol. 56 (1794), p. 624.

literary celebrity, but his fame had a rather unusual character. Some indication of the public's attitude is given by the "Advertisement" prefacing the third edition of the Wake (1814), in which the publisher is at pains to assure the reader "that The Queen's Wake is really and truly the production of James Hogg, a common shepherd". A Shepherd-Poet—like a Bearded Lady—was a curiosity, and Hogg's contemporary fame depended at least partly on his curiosity value.

As a result his writings were seldom judged objectively, without reference to the humble origins of their author. Hogg has an anecdote illustrating this in the final number of his periodical *The Spy* (24 August 1811). He tells how he copied some of the best essays of Addison and Johnson into his own handwriting, and showed them to various literary friends as his own productions. He goes on to say that "the Spy" "was soon convinced, to his utter astonishment, by arguments he could not controvert, that they were dull monotonous stuff; that the humour was coarse,—the grammar incorrect,—and that the philosophy contained in them was either inaccurate or inconsistent with common sense; and, in a word, that, besides being blurred with the most fulsome egotism, every sentence manifested a total ignorance of the principles of composition".

The picture of Hogg as an untutored child of nature was taken up by his friend John Wilson ("Christopher North") in the well known *Noctes Ambrosianae* of *Blackwood's Magazine*, in which Hogg appears as "the Ettrick Shepherd". The *Noctes*, which purport to be representations of the table-talk of the Blackwood group of writers, were in the main the work of Wilson, although other writers—including Hogg himself—also contributed. The series was extremely popular and as a result Hogg's name became well known throughout the English-speaking world.

The portrait of Hogg in the *Noctes* was not always flattering, and in 1831 he was vigorously defended in the *Quarterly Review* by Lockhart, who emphasised that Hogg was by no means the "boozing buffoon" portrayed in *Blackwood's*, and that in his adult years he had been "a laborious and successful student".[2] However, the impression made by the *Noctes* was a strong one, and when in 1832 Hogg visited London for the first and only time many people there were astonished at his unexpectedly civilised behaviour. William Howitt, for example, wrote: "Such was my own impression, derived

<hr>

[2] *Quarterly Review*, vol. 44 (1831), p. 82.

from this source [the *Noctes*], of Hogg, and from prints of him, with open mouth and huge straggling teeth, in full roars of drunken laughter, that, on meeting him in London, I was quite amazed to find him so smooth, well-looking, and gentlemanly a sort of person."[3]

Hogg's attitude towards the way he was portrayed in *Blackwood's* varied from anger to a good-natured enjoyment of the joke. In a letter to Scott of 1821 he says he is considering legal action as a result of a particularly outrageous review by Wilson of one of his books, and he goes on: "I am neither a drunkard nor an idiot nor a monster of nature. Nor am I so imbecile as never to have written a word of grammar in my life." In spite of his periodic angry outbursts, however, Hogg generally accepted his role as the butt of the Blackwood wits as the price to be paid for the enjoyment of what he called in one of his letters "their too much loved society".

He also enjoyed the wide publicity he received from the *Noctes*, and indeed he himself frequently set out to encourage the general interest in his character as a self-educated man of letters. Thus, on his visit to London he courted publicity by wearing a shepherd's plaid, and throughout his life he frequently referred to himself as "the Ettrick Shepherd".

Hogg also sought to arouse interest in himself by means of his autobiographical *Memoir of the Author's Life*, which gives a vivid account of his struggles first for literacy then for literary fame. The *Memoir* first appeared in 1807 in *The Mountain Bard*, a collection of his early verse which was prepared for publication with the help and encouragement of Scott. A new edition of *The Mountain Bard* appeared in 1821, and Hogg took the opportunity of bringing the *Memoir* up to date and of making some revisions. The *Memoir* was again revised and brought up to date in 1832 when it was published in *Altrive Tales*, the first volume of a projected twelve-volume edition of Hogg's prose. Hogg hoped the *Altrive Tales* would give financial security to his family after his death, but unfortunately only one volume appeared as the publisher, James Cochrane, became bankrupt. Three years after the *Altrive Tales* were published Hogg died, and the *Memoir* was reprinted posthumously as his "Autobiography" in the collected edition of his work edited by the Rev. T. Thomson and published in 1865. In the present edition the *Memoir* is reprinted from *Altrive Tales*, and the significant variations

---

[3] William Howitt, *Homes and haunts of the most eminent British Poets* (London, 1847), vol. 2, p. 37.

in the three texts published in Hogg's lifetime are recorded in footnotes.

Hogg's autobiography could scarcely fail to be interesting in view of the extraordinary circumstances of his life. It is also the most important single source of biographical information about him, and its interest is increased by the fact that it contains Hogg's reminiscences of contemporary literary figures, including Galt, Allan Cunningham, Lockhart and Wordsworth. Various attacks have been made on the accuracy of the *Memoir*, however. For example, George Goldie—the first publisher of *The Queen's Wake*—wrote of "the unblushing falsehoods which are so profusely interspersed in this notable piece of autobiography", and added that Hogg had "not only violated the confidence of friendship, but the sacredness of truth".[4] Where Hogg's veracity is open to doubt I have discussed the relevant evidence in footnotes or in the Commentary. Like many writers of autobiography Hogg sometimes falls short of complete objectivity and impartiality; thus Andrew Aikman could write with some justice "Mr Hogg, in the above, has given the truth, *but not all the truth*".[5] Equally, Hogg is frequently unreliable with regard to dates: for example, he states that he was born on 25 January 1772, yet his baptism in December 1770 is recorded in the Ettrick parish register. However, as Louis Simpson has said, "in its very errors and exaggerations the 'Autobiography' casts light upon Hogg's mind".

It is only fair to point out, however, that the extent and culpability of Hogg's inaccuracies in the *Memoir* have at times been exaggerated. Some of the evidence quoted in the notes and commentary confirms his truthfulness at points where his accuracy has been questioned, and none of the remaining "errors and exaggerations" appears to be seriously discreditable to Hogg. Indeed, some of the attacks which have been made on the *Memoir* border on the absurd. Thus Goldie describes Hogg's conversation with William Dunlop on *The Queen's Wake* (*Memoir*, p. 26) as "a story which wears such an appearance of low and vulgar blackguardism, that it is hard to believe it possible to have happened but between persons of the most abandoned habits. I particularly allude to the words put

---

[4] Goldie's attacks are contained in his *Letter to a Friend*, a pamphlet reply to Hogg's *Memoir* which was published after the appearance of the 1821 *Mountain Bard*, and which was reprinted in 1832 after the appearance of *Altrive Tales*.

[5] See Commentary.

into this gentelman's mouth. If any thing like this interview ever happened, no man who had any regard to decency or decorum himself, or valued these qualities in others, would, on any account, have defiled his pages with a detestable and revolting slang, equally offensive to pure religion and sound morals, and calculated even to degrade the nymphs of Billingsgate, or the pick-pockets of St Giles's." The only visible ground for Goldie's outburst is the fact that Dunlop jocularly calls Hogg a "useless poetical b——h", and later says "D——n your stupid head". One wonders what words Goldie would have found to give adequate expression to his disapproval of a more serious lapse in propriety.

A surprising feature of the *Memoir* is the fact that Hogg does not dwell on the deprivations of his childhood. Instead he recounts at length how he ran races against himself while herding cows, and how he caused alarm and amusement by playing the fiddle at night in his bed in a stable-loft. He mentions merely in passing that "from some of my masters I received very hard usage; in particular, while with one shepherd, I was often nearly exhausted with hunger and fatigue". This lack of bitterness and self-pity is an attractive quality, and indeed Hogg emerges from the *Memoir* as a man able to bear frequent misfortune and life-long poverty with courage and patience.

Hogg had intended for many years to write an account of Scott if he should outlive his friend, and two weeks after Scott's death in 1832 he wrote to Lockhart as follows:

My dear Lockhart
    Having been disappointed in seeing you at Kaeside which I hardly expected to do considering the confusion and distress you were in yet I cannot help writing to you thus early as I find that now having lost the best and most steady friend that I ever had in the world I have none now to depend on for advice or assistance but yourself. I never applied to anybody for these but to him and they never were wanting.
    I am thus going to begin by giving you a piece of advice. It is "That you will write Sir Walter's life in my name and in my manner" I think it will give you ten times more freedom of expression both as a critic and a friend and you know you can never speak too kindly of him for me. As I have promised such a thing to the world I really wish you would do it and I am sure it would take for there is no biographer alive equal to you but for a son brother or husband to write an original and interesting biography is impossible. Therefore be sure to take my name and forthright egotistical stile which you can well do and I think you

will not repent it. It will likwise do me some credit as a biographer and in fact there is no man can do it but you not having command of the documents. . . .[6]

The Blackwood group were in the habit of indulging in outrageous mystifications in print, one glorious example being Hogg's story in the *Memoir* of Lockhart and the Odontist. Lockhart did not take up this somewhat eccentric suggestion, however, and Hogg's next step was to undertake the task of writing his own reminiscences of Scott. He sent his completed manuscript to his London publisher Cochrane for the use of Cochrane's partner McCrone, who was preparing a life of Scott for publication. Hogg insisted that before publication his manuscript should be seen and edited by Lockhart, who was himself by this time at work on the "official" life of his father-in-law. Lockhart found Hogg's anecdotes outrageous and offensive, and expressed his opinion vigorously. Later in his *Life of Scott* he had this book in mind when he wrote of Hogg "it had been better for his fame had his end been of earlier date, for he did not follow his best benefactor until he had insulted his dust".

It has been said that Hogg was tactless in the *Familiar Anecdotes* when he speculated about the delicate subject of Lady Scott's parentage, and when he compared Scott's condition in the distressing final phase of his last illness to that of a drunken man. Similarly Hogg remarks upon Scott's "too strong leaning to the old aristocracy of the county", and this also may have offended Lockhart. These are the only passages in the *Familiar Anecdotes* to which Lockhart could reasonably have objected, however, and they scarcely constitute an insult to Scott's dust. Indeed, many passages in the book make Hogg's admiration and affection for Scott abundantly clear— "He was truly an extraordinary man; the greatest man in the world. What are kings and Emperors compared with him? Dust and sand!" In another passage Hogg writes that his anecdotes of Scott would be "trivial in the last degree did they not relate to so great and so good a man". Lockhart's anger can perhaps be interpreted as the distress of a man of aristocratic pretensions at finding the affairs of his father-in-law and of his own family discussed in print by a man of Hogg's lowly background.

A letter from Hogg to Cochrane of 12 May 1833 makes it clear

[6] Quoted by A. L. Strout in his "James Hogg's *Familiar Anecdotes of Sir Walter Scott*", *Studies in Philology*, vol. 33 (1934), p. 456.

that he had decided to give up his plans for publishing his reminiscences of Scott because of Lockhart's disapproval—

> I am sure I have no reason to be angry with you, though you may have some to be angry with me for withdrawing the manuscript which I wrote purposely for you, and at your request. But though I think Lockhart was very wrong, and behaved very ill, I do not see that I could behave otherwise than as I did. . . . I got a kind letter from Lockhart acknowledging that he had got into ill temper at our taking the start of him, and saying there were things in it that I durst not have published if Scott had been living. There he was wrong, for, saving for good friendship's sake, I cared as little either for Sir Walter's good or ill will as I do for his, though I have always considered myself honoured in both, and wish never to make an enemy whom I can retain as a friend. He asked pardon for any rash expression he might have used, but still he gave me no liberty to publish. I therefore think it would be better to suppress the work for a while. . . . I can add a great deal more, but I would not like to have these original anecdotes gambled, every one of which are strickly [sic] and literally true. They should either be published just fully and precisely as I have written them, or not at all. I got a tempting offer from a place called Albany, somewhere in America, for some original anecdotes of Scott, but I wrote an answer declining it. . . .[7]

This last sentence is perhaps a hint that Hogg would like Cochrane to agree to a transfer of his *Anecdotes* to Albany, in view of the fact that Lockhart's disapproval had made publication in Britain impracticable. In the event Hogg was able to write on 22 June 1833 to S. De Witt Bloodgood, his Albany correspondent, in these terms:

> There is such a genuine spirit of kindness in both your letters that I cannot resist complying with your request. I therefore send you the best article that I have in my own estimation. It was written for a young friend in London with a reference to Lockhart for correction, but he got into such a violent rage at my intrusion on his sphere that I thought proper to withdraw it. It is therefore wholly unappropriated and your own. I make you my trustee for it. Publish it in what shape or form or as many shapes or forms as you like. But attend to this. I would like if you would confine it to America, and not let the right of publishing reach Britain at all. But if you cannot effect this, and if it is contrary to the law of nations, then be sure to send every sheet as it comes from the press to Messrs Cochrane and Co., 11 Waterloo Place, London,

[7] This letter, and the following one, are quoted in W. S. Crockett, "The Shepherd's Sir Walter: Fresh Light on Hogg's Reminiscences", *The Glasgow Herald*, 22 Aug., 1931, p. 4, col. 2–4.

which secures the copyright to me here, provided the articles or work is published in London and Albany at the same time.

The *Familiar Anecdotes* were duly published by Harper and Brothers of New York in April 1834, with a memoir of Hogg by Bloodgood. In the following June a reprint of this book was published by John Reid & Co. of Glasgow, in association with Oliver & Boyd of Edinburgh and Whittaker, Treacher & Co. of London. This reprint was given the title *The Domestic Manners and Private Life of Sir Walter Scott*, and it includes a slightly shortened version of Bloodgood's memoir, as well as a number of new footnotes some of which are clearly not by Hogg.

As Hogg did not wish the *Anecdotes* to be published in Britain it seems clear that this was a pirated edition; indeed Cochrane had warned Hogg in a letter on 9 August 1833 that it was probable that any American edition would be followed quickly by a pirated British one.[8] Nevertheless, the work has usually been known as *The Domestic Manners*, and its text has invariably been reprinted from the British edition. In the present edition the text is reprinted from Hogg's manuscript, which survives in the Pierpoint Morgan Library, New York. A comparison of the printed text of the *Familiar Anecdotes* with the manuscript shows that a number of "improvements" have been made in Hogg's wording, presumably by Bloodgood. There are also some printers' errors.[9]

It has been suggested by both A. L. Strout and Miss E. C. Batho that Hogg revised the *Familiar Anecdotes* after McCrone had shown the manuscript to Lockhart, and that the published version represents the result of this revision. This theory is based on a passage from a letter written from London by William Blackwood in 1833. Blackwood gives an account of a conversation he had had with Lockhart, in which Lockhart referred to his talk with McCrone about Hogg's manuscript. Blackwood continues: "I had almost forgot to tell you a very curious part of the affair, though all in Hogg's own handwriting, it is given as if it were written by McCrone himself, and he takes good care to speak of himself in the laudatory way,

[8] National Library of Scotland MS. 2245, f. 230–1. The first writer to assert that the British edition was pirated was William Maginn in a review of *The Domestic Manners* in *Fraser's Magazine* (August 1834). Maginn used the evidence of dates to support his conclusion.

[9] These changes are listed and discussed by A. L. Strout in his "James Hogg's *Familiar Anecdotes of Sir Walter Scott*", *Studies in Philology*, vol. 33 (1934), p. 456–74.

as the excellent shepherd, the original genius &c &c &c and McCrone is supposed to write down the remarks of this son of genius, and most amusing colloquies are given betwixt the two worthies."[10]

Lockhart would certainly have told Blackwood that Hogg's manuscript was to be used by McCrone in the latter's proposed life of Scott. However, when Blackwood writes "it is given as if it were written by McCrone himself", this implies something more—that the manuscript Hogg sent to London was not written in the first person, as is the case in the published version. Hence Miss Batho and Strout conclude that some revision must have taken place before publication. This was probably the case, but perhaps it should be remembered that both Blackwood and Lockhart had quarreled with Hogg at this period, and that Blackwood was reporting a report of a manuscript which he had not himself seen; there was therefore some possibility of exaggeration and misunderstanding. Be that as it may, it seems unlikely that Hogg's revisions were extensive, in view of his unequivocal insistence to Cochrane that the anecdotes "should either be published just fully and precisely as I have written them, or not at all".

In a letter to Blackwood of 18 August 1834 Lockhart wrote:

> In Wilson's hands the Shepherd will always be delightful; but of the fellow himself I can scarcely express my contemptuous pity, now that his "Life of Sir W. Scott" is before the world. I believe it will, however, do Hogg more serious and lasting mischief than any of those whose feelings he has done his brutal best to lacerate would wish to be the result. He has drawn his own character, not that of his benevolent *creator*, and handed himself down to posterity—for the subject will keep *this* from being forgotten—as a mean blasphemer against all magnanimity. Poor Laidlaw will be mortified to the heart by this sad display. The bitterness against me which peeps out in many parts of Hogg's narrative is, of course, the fruit of certain rather hasty words spoken by me to Cochrane and MacCrone when they showed me the original MS, but nevertheless Hogg has *omitted* the only two passages which I had read when I so expressed myself,—one of them being a most flagrant assault on Scott's veracity, and the other a statement about poor Lady Scott, such as must have afflicted for ever her children, and especially her surviving daughter [i.e., Sophia, Lockhart's wife].[11]

[10] National Library of Scotland MS. 4035, f. 51–4. A somewhat different transcription is given by Mrs Oliphant in her *Annals of a Publishing House: William Blackwood and his Sons* (Edinburgh and London, 1897), vol. 2, p. 119–20.

[11] Quoted by E. C. Batho, *The Ettrick Shepherd* (Cambridge, 1927), p. 164.

In a letter to Hogg of 22 March 1833 Lockhart gives more details about the "statement about poor Lady Scott", which he describes as "your statement about Lady Scott and opium".[12] Nothing else, however, is known of what Hogg said in the two omitted passages, and it would not be safe to assume that they were as offensive as Lockhart implies; after all, Lockhart could describe Hogg's published anecdotes, which were at worst indiscreet, as an insult to Scott's dust. Indeed, nothing is known of Hogg's text or of the circumstances of its publication which would justify the severity of the criticism to which he has been subjected because of the *Familiar Anecdotes*. In fact the frankness which Lockhart found so disconcerting is for modern readers one of the chief attractions of the book. Hogg writes in the first paragraph "I shall in nothing extenuate or set down aught through partiality and as for malice that is out of the question", and his account of Scott "exactly as he was as he always appeared to me and was reported by others" has a humanity and freshness which could not have been achieved if he had adopted the expected tone of reverential hagiography.

Hogg's memoir of Scott, then, gives a first-hand account of a long friendship between two great writers, and as such it could scarcely fail to be interesting. Indeed, it throws a great deal of light on Hogg's own writings and personality as well as on those of Scott. It is also a deeply moving book in its closing pages, and especially in Hogg's quiet account of his last meeting with Scott in the autumn of 1830. Scott was already in the grip of his last illness.

> He then walked very ill indeed for the weak limb had become almost completely useless but he leaned on my shoulder all the way and did me the honour of saying that he never leaned on a firmer or a surer.
>
> We talked of many things past present and to come but both his memory and onward calculation appeared to me then to be considerably decayed. I cannot tell what it was but there was something in his manner that distressed me. He often changed the subject very abruptly and never laughed. He expressed the deepest concern for my welfare and success in life more than I had ever heard him do before and all mixed with sorrow for my worldly misfortunes. There is little doubt that his own were then preying on his vitals.

[12] Quoted by Francis R. Hart, *Lockhart as Romantic Biographer* (Edinburgh, 1971), p. 193. Hogg's surviving manuscript bears no traces of the omissions mentioned by Lockhart, nor of the revisions postulated by Strout and Miss Batho, and it seems likely that the manuscript which was sent to America was not the manuscript which had been sent to London.

There is a well-known and frequently quoted passage in Lockhart's *Life of Scott* in which a visit of Hogg to Castle Street is described. Hogg, who "bore most legible marks of a recent sheep-shearing", is represented as stretching himself full length on a sofa, to Mrs Scott's consternation. He "dined heartily and drank freely, and, by jest, anecdote, and song, afforded plentiful merriment to the more civilized part of the company . . . at supper, he fairly convulsed the whole party by addressing Mrs Scott as 'Charlotte' ". Sir Herbert Grierson has shown that Lockhart's *Life of Scott* contains "a somewhat surprising element of what appears to be sheer invention of a picturesque and dramatic character", and it seems possible that some of the picturesque details here are products of Lockhart's dramatic imagination—especially as this visit to Castle Street took place in 1803, fifteen years before Lockhart had met either Hogg or Scott.

In his authoritative *Sir Walter Scott: the Great Unknown* Edgar Johnson comments that in the *Life of Scott* Lockhart's "love of caricature led him to draw cruelly distorted pictures of Constable, the two Ballantynes, and James Hogg". Lockhart's picture of the unkempt buffoon reclining on Lady Scott's chintz has a good deal in common with Wilson's "Shepherd" of the *Noctes*, but for all their vigour these caricatures are scarcely adequate representations of the full complexity of the author of the *Confessions of a Justified Sinner*.

Hogg's public behaviour as "the Ettrick Shepherd" was at times grotesque; he was a vain man—as he himself often remarked; and on such occasions as the "triumphal arch scene" recorded in the *Memoir* he reacted somewhat too violently to denials of the worth of his hard-won accomplishments as a writer. Nevertheless, the *Memoir* and the *Familiar Anecdotes*, together with his other works, show him to have been a compassionate and quintessentially good-natured man. His friend R. P. Gillies remembered him thus in 1839: "His mild, reflective countenance, wore that expression which can only by given by contentment, and the '*mens sibi conscia recti*'. . . . He had great enjoyment of life; and, as Charles Lamb says of somebody, I forget who, 'his good-humour was catching'."[13]

Hogg has had many detractors, but he has always had some ready defenders. One of the ablest was Sir George Douglas, who in a

[13] R. P. Gillies, "Some Recollections of James Hogg", *Frazer's Magazine*, vol. 20 (1839), p. 420.

B

volume contributed to the *Famous Scots Series* in 1899 spoke of the need to do Hogg "that justice which hitherto has been but scantly meted out to him". Douglas's own estimate is perhaps the most just that has yet appeared:

> A figure so essentially strong and self-reliant is one to cherish and be proud of. Its ruggedness, its angles, are an essential part of it—it would not be itself without them. And then, if we turn to contemplate obstacles overcome, the great legend of the "pursuit of knowledge under difficulties"—a legend, as we venture to think, so particularly rich in Scotland—contains few stories more inspiring than Hogg's. And these stories are of the kind which gain greatly from the "happy ending." For, in all departments of life, it is only natural to salute the victor; and, though the Chattertons and David Grays may have aspired with equal generosity of feeling towards the light, we must allow its due of credit to the tougher fibre and the better balance which enabled Hogg to persevere until the goal was reached and the wreath wrested.[14]

If Hogg had merely become a competent writer in spite of the disadvantages of his childhood his achievement would have been admirable; that he should have been able to write works like "Kilmeny", "The Witch of Fife" and *The Private Memoirs and Confessions of a Justified Sinner* is perhaps an unparalleled example of the successful "pursuit of knowledge under difficulties".

[14] Sir George Douglas, *James Hogg* (Edinburgh and London, 1899), p. 120.

MEMOIR OF
THE AUTHOR'S LIFE

I LIKE to write about myself: in fact, there are few things which I like better; it is so delightful to call up old reminiscences. Often have I been laughed at for what an Edinburgh editor styles my good-natured egotism, which is sometimes any thing but that; and I am aware that I shall be laughed at again. But I care not: for this *important* Memoir, now to be brought forward for the fourth time,[1] at different periods of my life, I shall narrate with the same frankness as formerly; and in all, relating either to others or myself, speak fearlessly and unreservedly out. Many of those formerly mentioned are no more; others have been unfortunate; but of all I shall tell the plain truth, and nothing but the truth. So, without premising further, I shall proceed with an autobiography, containing much more of a romance than mere fancy could have suggested; and shall bring it forward to the very hour at which I am writing. The following note was prefixed by SIR WALTER SCOTT to the first edition of the Memoir in 1806.[2]

"THE friend to whom Mr. Hogg made the following communication had some hesitation in committing it to the public. On the one hand, he was sensible, not only that the incidents are often trivial, but that they are narrated in a style more suitable to their importance to the Author himself, than to their own nature and consequences. But the efforts of a strong mind and vigorous imagination, to develop themselves even under the most disadvantageous circumstances, may be always considered with pleasure, and often with profit; and if, upon a retrospect, the possessor be disposed to view with self-complacency his victory under difficulties, of which he only can judge the extent, it will be readily pardoned by those who consider the Author's scanty opportunities of knowledge,—and remember, that it is only on attaining the last and most recondite recess of human science, that we discover how little

[1] When Hogg states that the *Memoir* is "now to be brought forward for the fourth time" he seems to be including the two different issues of *The Mountain Bard* (both set from the same type) which appeared in 1807; the "third" edition of 1821; and the final version of the *Memoir* which appeared in *Altrive Tales* in 1832. The present edition follows the *Altrive Tales* text (hereafter quoted as AT). Significant variations between AT and the earlier texts are recorded in the footnotes.

[2] This first paragraph is not included in the versions of the *Memoir* printed in the 1807 and 1821 editions of *The Mountain Bard* (hereafter quoted as 07 and 21). 07 was in fact "the first edition of the Memoir"; Hogg no doubt gives the date 1806 because the letter to Scott which makes up the bulk of the 07 text is dated "Nov. 1806".

we really know. To those who are unacquainted with the pastoral scenes in which our Author was educated, it may afford some amusement to find real shepherds actually contending for a poetical prize, and to remark some other peculiarities in their habits and manners. Above all, these Memoirs ascertain the authenticity of the publication, and are therefore entitled to be prefixed to it."

MY DEAR SIR,[3]

According to your request, which I never disregard, I am now going to give you some account of my manner of life and *extensive* education. I must again apprize you, that, whenever I have occasion to speak of myself and my performances, I find it impossible to divest myself of an inherent vanity: but, making allowances for that, I will lay before you the outlines of my life,—with the circumstances that gave rise to my juvenile pieces, and my own opinion of them, as faithfully

> As if you were the minister of heaven
> Sent down to search the secret sins of men.

I am the second of four sons by the same father and mother; namely, Robert Hogg and Margaret Laidlaw, and was born on the 25th of January, 1772.[4] My progenitors were all shepherds of this country. My father, like myself, was bred to the occupation of a shepherd, and served in that capacity until his marriage with my mother; about which time, having saved a considerable sum of money, for those days, he took a lease of the farms of Ettrick House and Ettrick Hall. He then commenced dealing in sheep—bought up great numbers, and drove them both to the English and Scottish markets; but, at length, owing to a great fall in the price of sheep, and the absconding of his principal debtor, he was ruined, became bankrupt, every thing was sold by auction, and my parents were turned out of doors without a farthing in the world. I was then in the sixth year of my age, and remember well the distressed and destitute condition that we were in. At length the late worthy Mr.

---

[3] The first section of the *Memoir* takes the form of a letter addressed to Scott.

[4] *and was born ... 1772.* Added in AT. The Ettrick parish register shows that Hogg was mistaken about the date of his birth, as his baptism is recorded for 9 December 1770. It is interesting to note that Hogg convinced himself that he shared Burns's birthday, 25 January. However, his reasons for thinking he was born in 1772 are less obvious. "Dr Russell of Yarrow says that he was at last undeceived by the parish register and mourned over having two years less to live"—E. C. Batho, *The Ettrick Shepherd* (Cambridge, 1927), p. 11.

Brydon, of Crosslee, took compassion upon us; and, taking a short lease of the farm of Ettrick House, placed my father there as his shepherd, and thus afforded him the means of supporting us for a time. This gentleman continued to interest himself in our welfare until the day of his untimely death, when we lost the best friend that we had in the world.

At such an age, it cannot be expected that I should have made great progress in learning. The school-house, however, being almost at our door, I had attended it for a short time,[5] and had the honour of standing at the head of a juvenile class, who read the Shorter Catechism and the Proverbs of Solomon. At the next Whitsunday after our expulsion from the farm I was obliged to go to service; and, being only seven years of age, was hired by a farmer in the neighbourhood to herd a few cows; my wages for the half year being a ewe lamb and a pair of new shoes. Even at that early age my fancy seems to have been a hard neighbour for both judgment and memory. I was wont to strip off my clothes, and run races against time, or rather against myself; and, in the course of these exploits, which I accomplished much to my own admiration, I first lost my plaid, then my bonnet, then my coat, and, finally, my hosen; for, as for shoes, I had none. In that naked state did I herd for several days, till a shepherd and maid-servant were sent to the hills to look for them, and found them all.[6] Next year my parents took me home during the winter quarter, and put me to school with a lad named Ker, who was teaching the children of a neighbouring farmer. Here I advanced so far as to get into the class who read in the Bible. I had likewise, for some time before my quarter was out, tried writing; and had horribly defiled several sheets of paper with copy-lines, every letter of which was nearly an inch in length.

Thus terminated my education. After this I was never another day at any school whatever. In all I had spent about half a year at it. It is true, my former master denied this; and when I was only twenty years of age, said, if he was called on to make oath, he would swear I never was at his school. However, I know I was at it for two or three months; and I do not choose to be deprived of the honour of having attended the school of my native parish; nor yet that old John Beattie should lose the honour of such a scholar.[7] I was again, that

[5] *a short time* 07 "some time"; 21 as AT.

[6] *my wages for the half year . . . found them all.* Added in AT.

[7] *In all I had spent . . . such a scholar.* Not in 07. 21 as AT.

very spring, sent away to my old occupation of herding cows. This employment, the worst and lowest known in our country, I was engaged in for several years under sundry masters, till at length I got into the more honourable one of keeping sheep.

It will scarcely be believed that at so early an age I should have been an admirer of the other sex. It is nevertheless strictly true. Indeed I have liked the women a great deal better than the men ever since I remember. But that summer, when only eight years of age, I was sent out to a height called Broad-heads with a rosy-cheeked maiden to herd a flock of new-weaned lambs, and I had my mischievous cows to herd besides. But, as she had no dog and I had an excellent one, I was ordered to keep close by her. Never was a master's order better obeyed. Day after day I herded the cows and the lambs both, and Betty had nothing to do but to sit and sew. Then we dined together every day at a well near to the Shiel-sike head, and after dinner I laid my head down on her lap, covered her bare feet with my plaid, and pretended to fall sound asleep. One day I heard her say to herself, "Poor little laddie! he's joost tired to death," and then I wept till I was afraid she would feel the warm tears trickling on her knee. I wished my master, who was a handsome young man, would fall in love with her and marry her, wondering how he could be so blind and stupid as not to do it. But I thought if I were he, I would know well what to do.[8]

There is one circumstance which has led some to imagine that my abilities as a servant had not been exquisite; namely, that when I was fifteen years of age I had served a dozen masters; which circumstance I myself am rather willing to attribute to my having gone to service so young, that I was yearly growing stronger, and consequently adequate to a harder task and an increase of wages: for I do not remember of ever having served a master who refused giving me a verbal recommendation to the next, especially for my inoffensive behaviour. This character, which I, some way or other, got at my very first outset, has, in some degree, attended me ever since, and has certainly been of utility to me; yet, though Solomon avers that "a good name is rather to be chosen than great riches," I declare that I have never been so much benefited by mine, but that I would have chosen the latter by many degrees. From some of my masters I received very hard usage; in particular, while with one shepherd, I was often nearly exhausted with hunger and fatigue. All this while

---

[8] *It will scarcely be believed . . . what to do.*   Added in AT.

I neither read nor wrote; nor had I access to any book save the Bible. I was greatly taken with our version of the Psalms of David, learned the most of them by heart, and have a great partiality for them unto this day.[9] Every little pittance of wages that I earned was carried directly to my parents, who supplied me with what clothes I had. These were often scarcely worthy of the appellation. In particular, I remember being exceedingly bare of shirts: time after time I had but two, which often grew so bad that I was obliged to leave wearing them altogether. At these times I certainly made a very grotesque figure; for, on quitting the shirt, I could never induce my trews, or lower vestments, to keep up to their proper sphere, there being no braces in those days. When fourteen years of age I saved five shillings of my wages, with which I bought an old violin. This occupied all my leisure hours, and has been my favourite amusement ever since. I had commonly no spare time from labour during the day; but when I was not over-fatigued, I generally spent an hour or two every night in sawing over my favourite old Scottish tunes; and my bed being always in stables and cow-houses, I disturbed nobody but myself and my associate quadrupeds, whom I believed to be greatly delighted with my strains. At all events they never complained, which the biped part of my neighbours did frequently, to my pity and utter indignation.[10] This brings to my remembrance an anecdote, the consequence of one of these nocturnal endeavours at improvement.

When serving with Mr. Scott of Singlee, there happened to be a dance one evening, at which a number of the friends and neighbours of the family were present. I, being admitted into the room as a spectator, was all attention to the music; and, on the company breaking up, I retired to my stable-loft, and fell to essaying some of the tunes to which I had been listening. The musician going out to a short distance from the house,[11] and not being aware that another of the same craft was so near him, was not a little surprised when the tones of my old violin assailed his ears. At first he took it for the late warbles of his own ringing through his head; but, on a little

[9] The Church of Scotland's metrical Psalms. Hogg's love for this version of the Psalms is made clear in a letter he wrote in 1830 to the *Edinburgh Literary Journal* (vol. 3, p. 162–3). "I never read any poetry in my life that affected my heart half so much as those sublime strains of Zion, sung in what I conceived to be the pure spirit of their ancient simplicity; and the antiquated rhymes and Scotticisms at which Mr Tennant jeers so much, are to me quite endearing qualities."

[10] *and my associate quadrupeds . . . utter indignation.* Added in AT.

[11] *to a short distance from the house* 07 and 21 "on some necessary business".

attention, he, to his horror and astonishment, perceived that the sounds were real,—and that the tunes, which he had lately been playing with so much skill, were now murdered by some invisible being hard by him. Such a circumstance at that dead hour of the night, and when he was unable to discern from what quarter the sounds proceeded, convinced him all at once that it was a delusion of the devil; and, suspecting his intentions from so much familiarity, he fled precipitately into the hall, speechless with affright,[12] and in the utmost perturbation, to the no small mirth of Mr. Scott, who declared that he had lately been considerably annoyed himself by the same discordant sounds.

From Singlee I went to Elibank upon Tweed, where, with Mr. Laidlaw, I found my situation more easy and agreeable than it had ever yet been. I staid there three half-years—a term longer than usual; and from thence went to Willenslee, to Mr. Laidlaw's father, with whom I served as a shepherd two years,—having been for some seasons preceding employed in working with horses, threshing, &c.

It was while serving here, in the eighteenth year of my age, that I first got a perusal of "The Life and Adventures of Sir William Wallace,"[13] and "The Gentle Shepherd;"[14] and though immoderately fond of them, yet (what you will think remarkable in one who hath since dabbled so much in verse) I could not help regretting deeply that they were not in prose, that every body might have understood them; or, I thought if they had been in the same kind of metre with the Psalms, I could have borne with them. The truth is, I made exceedingly slow progress in reading them. The little reading that I had learned I had nearly lost, and the Scottish dialect quite confounded me; so that, before I got to the end of a line, I had commonly lost the rhyme of the preceding one; and if I came to a triplet, a thing of which I had no conception, I commonly read to the foot of the page without perceiving that I had lost the rhyme altogether. I thought the author had been straitened for rhymes, and had just made a part of it do as well as he could without them.[15]

---

[12] *speechless with affright*   07 and 21 "with disordered garments".

[13] By Blind Harry. Hogg probably read the poem in the paraphrase by William Hamilton of Gilbertfield, which was widely read in eighteenth-century Scotland, and which was also read with pleasure by the young Burns (see *The Letters of Robert Burns*, edited by J. de Lancey Ferguson (Oxford, 1931) letter 125).

[14] Allan Ramsay's pastoral comedy.

[15] *I thought the . . . without them.*   Not in 07; 21 as AT.

Thus, after I got through both works, I found myself much in the same predicament with the man of Eskdalemuir, who had borrowed Bailey's Dictionary[16] from his neighbour. On returning it, the lender asked him what he thought of it. "I dinna ken, man," replied he; "I have read it all through, but canna say that I understand it; it is the most confused book that ever I saw in my life!" The late Mrs. Laidlaw of Willenslee took some notice of me, and frequently gave me books to read while tending the ewes; these were chiefly theological. The only one, that I remember any thing of, is "Bishop Burnet's Theory of the Conflagration of the Earth."[17] Happy it was for me that I did not understand it! for the little of it that I did understand had nearly overturned my brain altogether. All the day I was pondering on the grand millennium, and the reign of the saints; and all the night dreaming of new heavens and a new earth —the stars in horror, and the world in flames! Mrs. Laidlaw also gave me sometimes the newspapers, which I pored on with great earnestness—beginning at the date, and reading straight on, through advertisements of houses and lands, balm of Gilead, and every thing; and, after all, was often no wiser than when I began. To give you some farther idea of the progress I had made in literature—I was about this time obliged to write a letter to my elder brother, and, having never drawn a pen for such a number of years, I had actually forgotten how to make sundry letters of the alphabet; these I had either to print, or to patch up the words in the best way I could without them.

At Whitsunday 1790, being still only in the eighteenth[18] year of my age, I left Willenslee, and hired myself to Mr. Laidlaw of Black House, with whom I served as a shepherd ten[19] years. The kindness of this gentleman to me it would be the utmost ingratitude in me ever to forget; for, indeed, it was much more like that of a father than a master,—and it is not improbable that I should have been there still, had it not been for the following circumstance.

[16] Nathan Bailey's dictionary (1721) was frequently reprinted in the eighteenth century, and was probably the most widely used English dictionary prior to Dr Johnson's.

[17] Hogg perhaps means *The Sacred Theory of the Earth* (1684), by Thomas Burnet (1635?–1715), a Yorkshire divine and master of the Charterhouse. Burnet's work was highly praised by Addison. Hogg may be confusing this Burnet, who was not a bishop, with the well known Bishop Gilbert Burnet (1643–1715).

[18] *eighteenth* 07 "nineteenth"; 21 as AT.

[19] *ten* 07 "nine"; 21 as AT.

My brother William had, for some time before, occupied the farm of Ettrick House, where he resided with our parents; but, having taken a wife, and the place not suiting two families, he took another residence, and gave up the farm to me. The lease expiring at Whitsunday 1803,[20] our possession was taken by a wealthier neighbour.

The first time that I attempted to write verses was in the spring of the year 1796.[21] Mr. Laidlaw having a number of valuable books, which were all open to my perusal, I about this time began to read with considerable attention;—and no sooner did I begin to read so as to understand, than, rather prematurely, I began to write. For several years my compositions consisted wholly of songs and ballads made up for the lasses to sing in chorus; and a proud man I was when I first heard the rosy nymphs chaunting my uncouth strains, and jeering me by the still dear appellation of "Jamie the poeter."[22]

I had no more difficulty in composing songs then than I have at present; and I was equally well pleased with them. But, then, the writing of them!—that was a job! I had no method of learning to write, save by following the Italian alphabet; and though I always stripped myself of coat and vest when I began to pen a song, yet my wrist took a cramp, so that I could rarely make above four or six lines at a sitting.[23] Whether my manner of writing it out was new, I know not, but it was not without singularity. Having very little spare time from my flock, which was unruly enough, I folded and stitched a few sheets of paper, which I carried in my pocket. I had no inkhorn; but, in place of it, I borrowed a small vial, which I fixed in a hole in the breast of my waistcoat; and having a cork fastened by a piece of twine, it answered the purpose fully as well. Thus equipped, whenever a leisure minute or two offered, and I had nothing else to

[20] 07 has "1793"; 21 as AT. There is clear evidence that 1793 is incorrect. In 07 the compositor's eye may have been caught by the "1793" in the next sentence (see following note).

[21] 07 and 21 have "1793". "Z", writing in the *Scots Magazine*, vol. 67 (1805), p. 502, also states that Hogg began to write verse in 1793. The evidence of Z is of particular interest as the unknown writer clearly obtained some of his information from Hogg himself (cf. E. C. Batho, *The Ettrick Shepherd* (Cambridge, 1927), p. 9–14). Hogg's first published work was a poem contributed anonymously to the *Scots Magazine* in 1794. His next publication, the song "Donald MacDonald", did not appear till 1800. Miss Batho (*The Ettrick Shepherd*, p. 13) has suggested that such changes as the substitution of 1796 for 1793 in AT are an attempt by Hogg "to make himself more interesting by extending the period of his illiteracy".

[22] *For several years . . . "Jamie the poeter."* This is inserted in AT in place of a longer passage in 07 and 21, which is reprinted in the Commentary.

[23] *I had no more difficulty . . . at a sitting.* Added in AT.

do, I sat down and wrote out my thoughts as I found them. This is still my invariable practice in writing prose. I cannot make out one sentence by study, without the pen in my hand to catch the ideas as they arise, and I never write two copies of the same thing.

My manner of composing poetry is very different, and, I believe, much more singular. Let the piece be of what length it will, I compose and correct it wholly in my mind, or on a slate, ere ever I put pen to paper; and then I write it down as fast as the A, B, C. When once it is written, it remains in that state; it being, as you very well know, with the utmost difficulty that I can be brought to alter one syllable, which I think is partly owing to the above practice.[24]

It is a fact, that, by a long acquaintance with any poetical piece, we become perfectly reconciled to its faults. The numbers, by being frequently repeated, wear smoother to our minds; and the ideas having been expanded, by our reflection on each particular scene or incident therein described, the mind cannot, without reluctance, consent to the alteration of any part of it.

The first time I ever heard of Burns was in 1797, the year after he died. One day during that summer a half daft man, named John Scott, came to me on the hill, and to amuse me repeated Tam O'Shanter. I was delighted! I was far more than delighted—I was ravished! I cannot describe my feelings; but, in short, before Jock Scott left me, I could recite the poem from beginning to end, and it has been my favourite poem ever since. He told me it was made by one Robert Burns, the sweetest poet that ever was born; but that he was now dead, and his place would never be supplied. He told me all about him, how he was born on the 25th of January, bred a ploughman, how many beautiful songs and poems he had composed, and that he had died last harvest, on the 21st of August.

This formed a new epoch of my life. Every day I pondered on the genius and fate of Burns. I wept, and always thought with myself— what is to hinder me from succeeding Burns? I too was born on the 25th of January, and I have much more time to read and compose than any ploughman could have, and can sing more old songs than ever ploughman could in the world. But then I wept again because I could not write. However, I resolved to be a poet, and to follow in the steps of Burns.

I remember in the year 1812, the year before the publication of

---

[24] As this was written for the 1807 edition it does not necessarily describe Hogg's later practice.

the "Queen's Wake," that I told my friend, the Rev. James Nicol, that I had an inward consciousness that I should yet live to be compared with Burns; and though I might never equal him in some things, I thought I might excel him in others. He reprobated the idea, and thought the assumption so audacious, that he told it as a bitter jest against me in a party that same evening. But the rest seeing me mortified, there was not one joined in the laugh against me, and Mr. John Grieve replied in these words, which I will never forget, "After what he has done, there is no man can say *what* he may do."[25]

My friend, Mr. William Laidlaw,[26] hath often remonstrated with me, in vain, on the necessity of a revisal of my pieces; but, in spite of him, I held fast my integrity: I said I would try to write the next better, but that should remain as it was. He was the only person who, for many years, ever pretended to discover the least merit in my essays, either in verse or prose; and, he never failed to have plenty of them about him, he took the opportunity of showing them to every person, whose capacity he supposed adequate to judge of their merits: but it was all to no purpose; he could make no proselytes to his opinion of any note, save one, who, in a little time, apostatized, and left us as we were. He even went so far as to break with some of his correspondents altogether, who persisted in their obstinacy. All this had not the least effect upon me; as long as I had his approbation and my own, which last never failed me, I continued to persevere. At length he had the good fortune to appeal to you,[27]

---

[25] *The first time I ever heard of Burns . . . he may do."* Not in 07 or 21. Burns in fact died on 21 July 1796, not 21 August 1796 as Hogg states. Miss E. C. Batho has pointed out that Hogg had published a poem in 1794, although here he states that he could not write in 1797. Dr Louis Simpson has commented "in saying that he could not write, Hogg may only mean that he found it difficult to do so". Donald Carswell describes Hogg's anecdote as "a . . . bare-faced lie", arguing that "every intelligent peasant in Scotland" had heard of Burns, and that Hogg would certainly have heard of him from the Laidlaws. Dr Simpson argues that "among people who are not literary . . . the names of authors are not particularly noted", and he concludes that "Hogg may be exaggerating—he was never loath to exaggerate—but the story seems acceptable in the main" (Louis Simpson, *James Hogg: a critical study* (Edinburgh and London, 1962)). The objections to the story seem to centre on the date Hogg assigns to it. Perhaps the incident described took place at an earlier date, and Hogg transferred it to the period immediately after Burns's death for artistic reasons. As we have seen, Hogg was not born on 25 January.

[26] The friend and amanuensis of Scott and steward of Abbotsford in later life. Laidlaw was the son of Mr Laidlaw of Blackhouse, Hogg's employer from 1790 to 1800.

[27] That is, Scott.

who were pleased to back him; and he came off triumphant, declaring, that the world should henceforth judge for themselves for him.

I have often opposed his proposals with such obstinacy, that I was afraid of losing his countenance altogether; but none of these things had the least effect upon him; his friendship continued unimpaired, attended with the most tender assiduities for my welfare; and I am now convinced that he is better acquainted with my nature and propensities than I am myself.

I have wandered insensibly from my subject: but to return.—In the spring of the year 1798,[28] as Alexander Laidlaw, a neighbouring shepherd, my brother William, and myself, were resting on the side of a hill above Ettrick church, I happened, in the course of our conversation, to drop some hints of my superior talents in poetry. William said, that, as to putting words into rhyme, it was a thing which he never could do to any sense; but that, if I liked to enter the lists with him in blank verse, he would take me up for any bet that I pleased. Laidlaw declared that he would venture likewise. This being settled, and the judges named, I accepted the challenge; but a dispute arising respecting the subject, we were obliged to resort to the following mode of decision: Ten subjects having been named, the lots were cast, and, amongst them all, that which fell to be elucidated by our matchless pens, was, *the stars!*—things which we knew little more about, than merely that they were burning and twinkling over us, and to be seen every night when the clouds were away. I began with high hopes and great warmth, and in a week declared my theme ready for the comparison; Laidlaw announced his next week; but my brother made us wait a full half year; and then, on being urged, presented his unfinished. The arbiters were then dispersed, and the cause was never properly judged; but those to whom they were shown rather gave the preference to my brother's. —This is certain, that it was far superior to either of the other two in the sublimity of the ideas; but, besides being in bad measure, it was often bombastical. The title of it was "Urania's Tour;" that of Laidlaw's, "Astronomical Thoughts;" and that of mine, "Reflections on a view of the Nocturnal Heavens."

Alexander Laidlaw and I tried, after the same manner, a paraphrase of the 117th Psalm, in English verse. I continued annually to add numbers of smaller pieces of poetry and songs to my collection,

[28] 07 and 21 have "1796".

mostly on subjects purely ideal, or else legendary. I had, from my childhood, been affected by the frequent return of a violent inward complaint;[29] and it attacked me once in a friend's house, at a distance from home, and, increasing to an inflammation, all hopes were given up of my recovery. While I was lying in the greatest agony, about the dead of the night, I had the mortification of seeing the old woman, who watched over me, fall into a swoon, from a supposition that she saw my *wraith*:—a spirit which, the vulgar suppose, haunts the abodes of such as are instantly to die, in order to carry off the soul as soon as it is disengaged from the body: and, next morning, I overheard a consultation about borrowing sheets to lay me in at my decease; but Almighty God, in his providence, deceived both them and the officious spirit; for, by the help of an able physician, I recovered, and have never since been troubled with the distemper.

My first published song was "Donald M'Donald," which I composed this year, 1800, on the threatened invasion by Buonaparte.[30] The first time I sung it was to a party of social friends at the Crown Tavern, Edinburgh. They commended it, on which I proffered it to one of them for his magazine. He said it was much too good for that, and advised me to give it to Mr. John Hamilton, who would set it to music and get it engraved. I did so, and went away again to the mountains, where I heard from day to day that the popularity of my song was unbounded, and yet no one ever knew or inquired who was the author.

There chanced to be about that time a great masonic meeting in Edinburgh, the Earl of Moira in the chair; on which occasion, Mr. Oliver, of the house of Oliver and Boyd, then one of the best singers in Scotland, sung "Donald M'Donald." It was loudly applauded, and three times encored; and so well pleased was Lord Moira with the song, that he rose, and in a long speech descanted on the utility of such songs at that period—thanked Mr. Oliver, and proffered him his whole interest in Scotland. This to the singer; yet, strange to say, he never inquired who was the author of the song!

There was at that period, and a number of years afterwards, a General M'Donald, who commanded the northern division of the British army. The song was sung at his mess every week-day, and sometimes twice and thrice. The old man was proud of, and delighted

---

[29] *inward complaint*   07 and 21 have "pain in my bowels".

[30] Hogg had contributed "The Mistakes of a Night" anonymously to *The Scots Magazine* in 1794. "Donald MacDonald" in 1800 was thus his second publication.

in it, and was wont to snap his thumbs and join in the chorus. He believed, to his dying day, that it was made upon himself; yet neither he nor one of his officers ever knew or inquired who was the author—so thankless is the poet's trade! It was, perhaps, the most popular song that ever was written. For many other comical anecdotes relating to it, see a collection of my songs published by Mr. Blackwood last year.[31]

In 1801, believing that I was then become a grand poet, I most sapiently determined on publishing a pamphlet, and appealing to the world at once. This noble resolution was no sooner taken than executed; a proceeding much of a piece with many of my subsequent transactions.[32] Having attended the Edinburgh market one Monday, with a number of sheep for sale, and being unable to dispose of them all, I put the remainder into a park until the market on Wednesday. Not knowing how to pass the interim, it came into my head that I would write a poem or two from my memory, and get them printed. The thought had no sooner struck me than it was put in practice; and I was obliged to select, not the best poems, but those that I remembered best. I wrote several of these during my short stay, and gave them all to a person to print at my expense, and, having sold off my sheep on Wednesday morning, I returned to the Forest. I saw no more of my poems until I received word that there were one thousand copies of them thrown off. I knew no more about publishing than the man of the moon; and the only motive that influenced me was, the gratification of my vanity by seeing my works in print. But, no sooner did the first copy come to hand, than my eyes were open to the folly of my conduct; for, on comparing it with the MS. which I had at home, I found many of the stanzas omitted, others misplaced, and typographical errors abounding in every page.[33]

Thus were my first productions pushed headlong into the world, without either patron or preface, or even apprising the public that such a thing was coming, and "unhousell'd, unanointed, unaneled, with all their imperfections on their heads." "Will an' Keatie," however, had the honour of being copied into some periodical pub-

---

[31] *Songs, by the Ettrick Shepherd* (Edinburgh and London, 1831). The "other comical anecdotes" are reprinted in my edition of Hogg's *Selected Poems* (Oxford, 1970).

[32] *My first published song was "Donald M'Donald,"* ... *my subsequent transactions.* Not in 07 or 21, which have instead information on other early works. See Commentary.

[33] *abounding in every page.* 07 "were without number"; 21 as AT.

C

lications of the time, as a favourable specimen of the work. Indeed, all of them were sad stuff, although I judged them to be exceedingly good.

The truth was, that, notwithstanding my pride of authorship, in a few days I had discernment enough left to wish my publication heartily at the devil, and I had hopes that long ago it had been consigned to eternal oblivion; when, behold! a London critic had in malice of heart preserved a copy, and quoted liberally out of it last year, to my intense chagrin and mortification.

On the appearance of "The Minstrelsy of the Scottish Border," I was much dissatisfied with the imitations of the ancient ballads contained in it, and immediately set about imitating the ancient ballads myself—selected a number of traditionary stories, and put them in metre by chanting them to certain old tunes. In these I was more successful than in any thing I had hitherto tried, although they were still but rude pieces of composition.[34]

THE above is the substance of three letters, written in the same year, and alluding mostly to Poetical Trifles. Since that time I have experienced a very unexpected reverse of fortune. After my return from the Highlands in June last, I put every thing in readiness for my departure to settle in Harris;[35] and I wrote and published my "Farewell to Ettrick," wherein the real sentiments of my heart at that time are simply related, which constitute[36] its only claim to merit. It would be tedious and trifling, were I to relate all the dis-

---

[34] *Indeed, all of them were sad stuff . . . composition.* Not in 07 or 21, which have instead a long passage not in AT. See Commentary. Hogg overstates the typographical imperfections of *Scottish Pastorals,* and it is known that he had an opportunity to revise proofs of the book (see A. L. Strout, *The Life and Letters of James Hogg* (1946), p. 24–8). Strout also reprints here a letter "evidently not by Hogg himself" which "bears out his claim that his first volume was unpremeditated". This letter describes how the poems were written from memory in the printer's shop in the Grassmarket. T. Craig-Brown, in his *History of Selkirkshire* (Edinburgh, 1886), p. 341, argues that the poems could not have been written from memory as Hogg claims, because Hogg wrote to Laidlaw after publication "As for the wrong insertion of Lord Napier's name I now see my error, but what the devil in hell, as I should say so, ailed both you and Clarkson, who had both perused the manuscript, that you had not told me that sooner." However, the fact that Laidlaw and Clarkson had seen the manuscript before publication does not necessarily prove that Hogg had the manuscript with him in Edinburgh when he went to the printer.

[35] In 1804 Hogg intended to move with his parents to a sheep farm in Harris, but was refused possession of the farm because of a legal complication.

[36] 07 "probably, constitute". 21 as AT.

agreeable circumstances which ensued; suffice it to say, that my scheme was absolutely frustrated.

Miserably disappointed, and vexed at having been thus baffled in an undertaking about which I had talked so much, to avoid a great many disagreeable questions and explanations, I went to England during the remainder of the summer.[37] On my return to Scotland, having lost all the money that I had made by a regular and industrious life, and in one week too, I again cheerfully hired myself as a shepherd, with Mr. Harkness of Mitchell-Slack, in Nithsdale. It was while here that I published "The Mountain Bard," consisting of the above-mentioned ballads.[38] Sir Walter, then Mr. Scott, had encouraged the publication of the work in some letters that he sent me; consequently I went to Edinburgh to see about it. He went with me to Mr. Constable, who received me very kindly, but told me frankly that my poetry would not sell. I said I thought it was as good as any body's I had seen. He said that might be, but that nobody's poetry would sell; it was the worst stuff that came to market, and that he found; but, as I appeared to be a gay, queer chiel, if I would procure him two hundred subscribers he would publish my work for me, and give me as much for it as he could. I did not like the subscribers much; but, having no alternative, I accepted the conditions. Before the work was ready for publication I had got above five hundred subscribers; and Mr. Constable, who, by that time, had conceived a better opinion of the work, gave me half-guinea copies for all my subscribers, and a letter for a small sum over and above. I have forgot how much; but, upon the whole, he acted with great liberality. He gave me, likewise, that same year, eighty-six pounds for that celebrated work, "Hogg on Sheep;"[39] and I was now richer than I had ever been before.

I had no regular plan of delivering those copies that were subscribed for, but sent them simply to the people, intending to take their money in return; but though some paid me double, triple, and even ten times the price, about one-third of my subscribers thought

[37] In 07 an extra passage is inserted here, after which 07 ends. See Commentary. 21 as AT.

[38] "The Mountain Bard" ... ballads. 21 " 'The Mountain Bard,' containing all the ballads which follow, save a very few, and such other poems and songs as I liked best, to make it a reasonable size."

[39] The Shepherd's Guide: being a practical treatise on the diseases of sheep (Edinburgh, Archibald Constable and Co., 1807).

proper to take the copies for nothing, never paying for them to this day.

Being now master of nearly three hundred pounds, I went perfectly mad. I first took one pasture farm, at exactly one half more than it was worth, having been cheated into it by a great rascal, who meant to rob me of all I had, and which, in the course of one year, he effected by dint of law. But, in the mean time, having taken another extensive farm, I found myself fairly involved in business far above my capital. It would have required at least one thousand pounds for every one hundred pounds that I possessed, to have managed all I had taken in hand; so I got every day out of one strait and confusion into a worse. I blundered and struggled on for three years between these two places, giving up all thoughts of poetry or literature of any kind. I have detailed these circumstances in a larger MS. work; but, though they are most laughable, they must be omitted here, as it is only a short sketch of my *literary life* that I can include in this introduction.

Finding myself, at length, fairly run aground, I gave my creditors all that I had, or rather suffered them to take it, and came off and left them. I never asked any settlement, which would not have been refused me; and severely have I smarted for that neglect since. None of these matters had the least effect in depressing my spirits—I was generally rather most cheerful when most unfortunate. On returning again to Ettrick Forest, I found the countenances of all my friends altered; and even those whom I had loved, and trusted most, disowned me, and told me so to my face; but I laughed at and despised these persons, resolving to show them, by and by, that they were in the wrong. Having appeared as a poet, and a speculative farmer besides, no one would now employ me as a shepherd. I even applied to some of my old masters, but they refused me, and for a whole winter I found myself without employment, and without money, in my native country; therefore, in February 1810, in utter desperation, I took my plaid about my shoulders, and marched away to Edinburgh, determined, since no better could be, to push my fortune as a literary man. It is true, I had estimated my poetical talent high enough, but I had resolved to use it only as a staff, never as a crutch; and would have kept that resolve, had I not been driven to the reverse. On going to Edinburgh, I found that my poetical talents were rated nearly as low there as my shepherd qualities were in Ettrick. It was in vain that I applied to newsmongers, booksellers, editors of magazines, &c. for employment. Any of these were willing enough to accept of my lucubrations, and give them publicity, but then there was no money going—not a farthing; and this suited me very ill.

I again applied to Mr. Constable, to publish a volume of songs for me; for I had nothing else by me but the songs of my youth, having given up all these exercises so long. He was rather averse to the expedient; but he had a sort of kindness for me, and did not like to refuse; so, after waiting on him three or four times, he agreed to print an edition, and give me half the profits. He published one thousand copies, at five shillings each; but he never gave me any thing; and as I feared the concern might not have proved a good one, I never asked any remuneration.

The name of this work was "The Forest Minstrel;" of which about two-thirds of the songs were my own, the rest furnished by correspondents—a number of them by the ingenious Mr. T. M. Cunningham. In general they are not good, but the worst of them are all mine, for I inserted every ranting rhyme that I had made in my youth, to please the circles about the firesides in the country; and all this time I had never been once in any polished society— had read next to nothing—was now in the 38th year of my age—and knew no more of human life or manners than a child. I was a sort of natural songster, without another advantage on earth. Fain would I have done something; but, on finding myself shunned by every one, I determined to push my own fortune independent of booksellers, whom I now began to view as enemies to all genius. My plan was, to begin a literary weekly paper, a work for which I certainly was rarely qualified, when the above facts are considered. I tried Walker and Greig, and several printers, offering them security to print it for me.—No; not one of them would print it without a bookseller's name to it as publisher. "D——n them," said I to myself, as I was running from one to another, "the folks here are all combined in a body." Mr. Constable laughed at me exceedingly, and finally told me he wished me too well to encourage such a thing. Mr. Ballantyne[40] was rather more civil, and got off by subscribing for so many copies, and giving me credit for ten pounds worth of paper. David Brown would have nothing to do with it, unless some gentleman,[41]

[40] The brothers James and John Ballantyne were the business associates of Scott. Hogg mentions the brothers frequently.

[41] 21 "gentlemen,".

whom he named, should contribute. At length, I found an honest man, James Robertson, a bookseller in Nicolson Street, whom I had never before seen or heard of, who undertook it at once on my own terms; and on the 1st of September, 1810, my first number made its appearance on a quarto demy sheet, price fourpence.[42]

A great number were sold, and many hundreds delivered gratis; but one of Robertson's boys, a great rascal, had demanded the price in full for all that he was to have delivered gratis. They showed him the imprint, that they were to be delivered gratis: "So they are," said he; "I take nothing for the delivery; but I must have the price of the paper, if you please."

This money that the boy brought me, consisting of a few shillings and an immense number of halfpence, was the first and only money I had pocketed of my own making since my arrival in Edinburgh in February. On the publication of the first two numbers, I deemed I had as many subscribers as, at all events, would secure the work from being dropped; but, on the publication of my third or fourth number, I have forgot which, it was so indecorous, that no fewer than seventy-three subscribers gave up. This was a sad blow for me; but, as usual, I despised the fastidiousness and affectation of the people, and continued my work. It proved a fatal oversight for the paper, for all those who had given in set themselves against it with the utmost inveteracy. The literary ladies, in particular, agreed, in full divan, that I would never write a sentence which deserved to be read. A reverend friend of mine has often repeated my remark on being told of this—"Gaping deevils! wha cares what they say? If I leeve ony time, I'll let them see the contrair o' that."

My publisher, James Robertson, was a kind-hearted, confused body, who loved a joke and a dram. He sent for me every day about one o'clock, to consult about the publication; and then we uniformly went down to a dark house in the Cowgate, where we drank whisky and ate rolls with a number of printers, the dirtiest and leanest-looking men I had ever seen. My youthful habits having been so regular, I could not stand this; and though I took care, as I thought, to drink very little, yet, when I went out, I was at times so dizzy, I could scarcely walk; and the worst thing of all was, I felt that I was beginning to relish it.

Whenever a man thinks seriously of a thing, he generally thinks aright. I thought frequently of these habits and connexions, and

[42] The title of Hogg's periodical was *The Spy*.

found that they never would do; and that, instead of pushing myself forward, as I wished, I was going straight to the devil. I said nothing about this to my respectable acquaintances, nor do I know if they ever knew or suspected what was going on; but, on some pretence or other, I resolved to cut all connexion with Robertson; and, sorely against his will, gave the printing to the Messrs. Aikman, then proprietors of the Star newspaper, showing them the list of subscribers, of which they took their chance, and promised me half profits. At the conclusion of the year, instead of granting me any profits, they complained of being minus, and charged me with the half of the loss. This I refused to pay, unless they could give me an account of all the numbers published, on the sale of which there should have been a good profit. This they could not do; so I paid nothing, and received as little.[43] I had, however, a good deal to pay to Robertson, who likewise asked more; so that, after a year's literary drudgery, I found myself a loser rather than a gainer.

The name of this periodical work was "The Spy." I continued it for a year, and to this day I cannot help regarding it as a literary curiosity. It has, doubtless, but little merit; but yet I think that, all circumstances considered, it is rather wonderful. In my farewell paper I see the following sentence occurs, when speaking of the few who stood friends to the work:—

"They have, at all events, the honour of patronising an undertaking quite new in the records of literature; for, that a common shepherd, who never was at school; who went to service at seven years of age, and could neither read nor write with any degree of accuracy when thirty;[44] yet who, smitten with an unconquerable thirst after knowledge, should leave his native mountains,[45] and his flocks to wander where they chose, come to the metropolis with his plaid wrapped about his shoulders, and all at once set up for a connoisseur in manners, taste, and genius—has much more the appearance of a romance than a matter of fact; yet a matter of fact it certainly is;—and such a person is the editor of 'The Spy.' "

I begun it without asking, or knowing of any assistance; but when

---

[43] According to Andrew Aikman, one of the Messrs Aikman, Hogg here "has given the truth, but not all the truth". Aikman's account is reprinted in the Commentary.

[44] 21 has "twenty", which is also the reading of *The Spy*.

[45] *should leave his native mountains* In *The Spy* this reads " . . . should run away from his master, leave his native mountains . . .".

Mr. and Mrs. Gray[46] saw it was on foot, they interested themselves in it with all their power, and wrote a number of essays for it. Several other gentlemen likewise contributed a paper quietly now and then, and among others Robert Sym, Esq., which I never discovered till after the work was discontinued. Professor T. Gillespie, the Rev. Wm. Gillespie, J. Black of the Morning Chronicle, and sundry others, lent me an occasional lift. The greater part, however, is my own writing, and consists of four hundred and fifteen quarto pages, double columned,—no easy task for one person to accomplish in a year. I speak of this work as of one that *existed*, for it flew abroad, like the sibyl's papers, every week, and I believe there are not above five complete copies existing, if indeed there is one;[47] and, as it never will be reprinted, if the scarcity of a work makes it valuable, no one can be more so, to exist at all.

All this while there was no man who entered into my views, and supported them, save Mr. John Grieve,[48] a friend, whose affection neither misfortune nor imprudence could once shake. Evil speakers had no effect on him. We had been acquainted from our youth; and he had formed his judgment of me as a man and a poet; and from that nothing could ever make him abate one item. Mr. Grieve's opinion of me was by far too partial, for it amounted to this, that he never conceived any effort in poetry above my reach, if I would set my mind to it; but my carelessness and indifference he constantly regretted and deprecated. During the first six months that I resided in Edinburgh I lived with him, and his partner, Mr. Scott, who, on a longer acquaintance, became as firmly attached to me as Mr. Grieve; and, I believe, as much so as to any other man alive. We three have had many very happy evenings together; we indeed were seldom separate when it was possible to meet. They suffered me to want for nothing, either in money or clothes; and I did not even need to ask these. Mr. Grieve was always the first to notice my wants, and prevent them. In short, they would not suffer me to be obliged

---

[46] James Gray, of Edinburgh High School. In 1820 Hogg married the sister of Gray's first wife.

[47] *if indeed there is one* Added in AT. Fewer than ten complete sets of *The Spy* now exist (see G. H. Bushnell, " 'The Spy': James Hogg's adventure in journalism", *Scots Magazine*, NS vol. 36 (1941), p. 197–205). *The Spy* consists of 52 numbers, and there are complete sets in the National Library of Scotland and St Andrews University Library.

[48] Grieve was a hatter, with premises on the North Bridge. He was a man of real literary taste, and gave help to a number of struggling authors. Hogg dedicated his long poem *Mador of the Moor* to Grieve.

to any one but themselves for the value of a farthing; and without
this sure support I could never have fought my way in Edinburgh.
I was fairly starved into it, and if it had not been for Messrs. Grieve
and Scott, would, in a very short time, have been starved out of it
again.

The next thing in which I became deeply interested, in a literary
way, was the FORUM, a debating society, established by a few young
men, of whom I, though far from being a young man, was one of the
first. We opened our house to the public, making each individual
pay a sixpence, and the crowds that attended, for three years run
ning, were beyond all bounds. I was appointed secretary, with a
salary of twenty pounds a year, which never was paid, though I gave
away hundreds in charity. We were exceedingly improvident; but I
never was so much advantaged by any thing as by that society; for
it let me feel, as it were, the pulse of the public, and precisely what
they would swallow, and what they would not. All my friends were
averse to my coming forward in the Forum as a public speaker, and
tried to reason me out of it, by representing my incapacity to
harangue a thousand people in a speech of half an hour. I had,
however, given my word to my associates, and my confidence in
myself being unbounded, I began, and came off with flying colours.
We met once a week. I spoke every night, and sometimes twice the
same night; and, though I sometimes incurred pointed disapprobation, was in general a prodigious favourite. The characters of all my
brother members are given in the larger work, but here they import
not. I have scarcely known any society of young men who have all
got so well on. Their progress has been singular; and, I am certain,
people may say what they will, that they were greatly improved by
their weekly appearances in the Forum. Private societies signify
nothing; but a discerning public is a severe test, especially in a
multitude, where the smallest departure from good taste, or from
the question, was sure to draw down disapproval, and where no good
saying ever missed observation and applause. If this do not assist in
improving the taste, I know not what will. Of this I am certain, that
I was greatly the better for it, and I may safely say I never was in a
school before. I might and would have written the "Queen's Wake"
had the Forum never existed, but without the weekly lessons that I
got there I could not have succeeded as I did. Still our meetings
were somewhat ludicrous, especially the formality of some of the
presidents. To me they were so irresistible, that I wrote a musical

farce, in three acts, called "The Forum, a Tragedy for Cold Weather," wherein all the members are broadly taken off, myself not excepted, and some of our evening scenes depicted. I believe it is a good thing of the kind, at least I remember thinking so at the time; but it was so severe on some of my friends, who had a few peculiarities about them, that I never showed it to any one. I have it by me; but I believe never man saw it save myself. About the same time I wrote another musical drama of three acts, and showed it to Mr. Siddons.[49] He approved of it very highly, with the exception of some trivial scene, which I promised to alter, and he undertook to have it acted on the return of the season; but I never saw him again. He was always kind and friendly to me, and made me free to the theatre from year to year.

During the time that the Forum was going on the poetry of Mr. Walter Scott and Lord Byron was exciting general attention. I had published some pieces in "The Spy" that Grieve thought exceedingly good; and nothing would serve him but that I should take the field once more as a poet, and try my fate with others. I promised; and having some ballads or metrical tales by me, which I did not like to lose, I planned the "Queen's Wake," in order that I might take these all in, and had it ready in a few months after it was first proposed. I was very anxious to read it to some person of taste; but no one would either read it, or listen to my reading it, save Grieve, who assured me it would do. As I lived at Deanhaugh then, I invited Mr. and Mrs. Gray to drink tea, and to read a part of it with me before offering it for publication. Unluckily, however, before I had read half a page, Mrs. Gray objected to a word, which Grieve approved of and defended, and some high disputes arose; other authors were appealed to, and notwithstanding my giving several very broad hints, I could not procure a hearing for another line of my new poem. Indeed, I was sorely disappointed, and told my friends so on going away; on which another day was appointed, and I took my manuscript to Buccleuch Place. Mr. Gray had not got through the third page when he was told that an itinerant bard had entered the lobby, and was repeating his poetry to the boarders. Mr. Gray went out and joined them, leaving me alone with a young lady, to read, or not, as we liked. In about half an hour he sent a request for me likewise to come: on which I went, and heard a poor crazy

[49] Henry Siddons, son of the renowned Sarah Siddons, and manager of the Edinburgh Theatre, of which Scott was a trustee.

beggar repeating such miserable stuff as I had never heard before. I was terribly affronted; and putting my manuscript in my pocket, I jogged my way home in very bad humour. Gray has sometimes tried to deny the truth of this anecdote, and to face me out of it, but it would not do. I never estimated him the less as a friend; but I did not forget it, in one point of view; for I never read any more new poems to him.

I next went to my friend Mr. Constable, and told him my plan of publication; but he received me coldly, and told me to call again. I did so—when he said he would do nothing until he had seen the MS. I refused to give it, saying, "What skill have you about the merits of a book?"—"It may be so, Hogg," said he; "but I know as well how to sell a book as any man, which should be some concern of yours; and I know how to buy one, too, by G——!"

Finally, he told me, that if I would procure him two hundred subscribers, to insure him from loss, he would give me £100 for liberty to print one thousand copies; and more than that he would not give. I felt I should be obliged to comply; and, with great reluctance, got a few subscription-papers thrown off privately, and gave them to friends, who soon procured me the requisite number. But, before this time, one George Goldie, a young bookseller in Princes Street, a lad of some taste, had become acquainted with me at the Forum, and earnestly requested to see my MS. I gave it to him with reluctance, being predetermined to have nothing to do with him. He had not, however, well looked into the work till he thought he perceived something above common-place; and, when I next saw him, he was intent on being the publisher of the work, offering me as much as Mr. Constable, and all the subscribers to myself over and above. I was very loath to part with Mr. Constable; but the terms were so different, that I was obliged to think of it. I tried him again; but he had differed with Mr. Scott, and I found him in such bad humour, that he would do nothing farther than curse all the poets, and declare that he had met with more ingratitude from literary men than all the rest of the human race. Of course Goldie got the work, and it made its appearance in the spring of 1813.[50]

As I said, nobody had seen the work; and, on the day after it was published, I went up to Edinburgh as anxious as a man could be.

---

[50] Hogg's account of the publication of *The Queen's Wake* was vigorously disputed by Goldie, who also disputed some of Hogg's statements about the Forum. Goldie's evidence is summarised and discussed in the Commentary.

I walked sometimes about the streets, and read the title of my book on the booksellers' windows, yet I durst not go into any of the shops. I was like a man between death and life, waiting for the sentence of the jury. The first encouragement that I got was from my country-man, Mr. William Dunlop, wine and spirit merchant, who, on observing me going sauntering up the plainstones of the High Street, came over from the Cross, arm-in-arm with another gentleman, a stranger to me. I remember his salutation, word for word; and, singular as it was, it made a strong impression; for I knew that Mr. Dunlop had a great deal of rough common sense.

"Ye useless poetical deevil[51] that ye 're!" said he, "what hae ye been doing a' this time?"—"What doing, Willie! what do you mean?"—"D——n your stupid head, ye hae been pestering us wi' fourpenny papers an' daft shilly-shally sangs, an' bletherin' an' speakin' i' the Forum, an' yet had stuff in ye to produce a thing like this!"—"Ay, Willie," said I; "have you seen my new beuk?"—"Ay, faith, that I have, man; and it has lickit me out o' a night's sleep. Ye hae hit the right nail on the head now. Yon 's the very thing, sir."—"I'm very glad to hear you say sae, Willie; but what do ye ken about poems?"—"Never ye mind how I ken; I gi'e you my word for it, yon's the thing that will do. If ye hadna made a fool o' yoursel' afore, man, yon wad hae sold better than ever a book sold. Od, wha wad hae thought there was as muckle in that sheep's-head o' yours?—d——d stupid poetical deevil[52] that ye're!" And with that he went away, laughing and miscalling me over his shoulder.

This address gave me a little confidence, and I faced my acquain-tances one by one; and every thing that I heard was laudatory. The first report of any work that goes abroad, be it good or bad, spreads like fire set to a hill of heather in a warm spring day, and no one knows where it will stop. From that day forward every one has spoken well of the work; and every review praised its general fea-tures, save the Eclectic, which, in the year 1813, tried to hold it up to ridicule and contempt. Mr. Jeffery[53] ventured not a word about

---

[51] 21 has "b——h". " 'Bitch' was not then applied only to females: Lord Kames, on retiring from the Court of Session, had looked back from the doorway at his former colleagues and cried heartily, 'Fare ye a' weel, ye bitches!' " (Edgar Johnson, *Sir Walter Scott: the Great Unknown* (London, 1970), p. 95).

[52] 21 has "b——h".

[53] Francis Jeffrey (1773–1850), editor of the *Edinburgh Review* and perhaps the most influential reviewer of the period. The *Edinburgh Review* was Whig in politics, while

it, either good or bad, himself, until the year after, when it had fairly got into a second and third edition. He then gave a very judicious and sensible review of it; but he committed a most horrible blunder, in classing Mr. Tenant, the author of "Anster Fair," and me together, as two self-taught geniuses; whereas there was not one point of resemblance. Tenant being a better educated man than the reviewer himself, was not a little affronted at being classed with me.[54] From that day to this Mr. Jeffery has taken no notice of any thing that I have published, which I think can hardly be expected to do him any honour at the long run. I should like the worst poem that I have since published to stand a fair comparison with some that he has strained himself to bring forward. It is a pity that any literary connexion, which with the one party might be unavoidable, should ever prejudice one valued friend and acquaintance against another. In the heart-burnings of party spirit, the failings of great minds are more exposed than in all other things in the world put together.

Mr. Goldie had little capital, and less interest among the trade; nevertheless, he did all for my work that lay in his power, and sold two editions of it in a short time. About that period a general failure took place among the secondary class of booksellers, and it was reported that Goldie was so much involved with some of the houses, that it was impossible he could escape destruction. A third edition of my poem was wanted, and, without more ado, I went and offered it to Mr. Constable. We closed a bargain at once, and the book was sent to Mr. Ballantyne to print. But after a part was thrown off, Goldie got notice of the transaction, and was neither to hold nor bind, pretending that he had been exceedingly ill used. He waited on Mr. Constable one hour, and corresponded with him the next,

---

Hogg was associated with the Tory *Blackwood's Magazine*. Hogg consistently spells Jeffrey's name "Jeffery" in AT.

[54] "Mr Jeffrey committed no such 'blunder,' as he is here accused of. 'The Queen's Wake' and 'Anster Fair' were reviewed in the same number of the *Edinburgh Review, in separate articles*. The authors were spoken of as both originally belonging to an humble condition of life, but no further parallel was drawn between them. Mr. Tennant's scholarship is not over-looked in the *Review*: on the contrary, he is recognized as being a 'distinguished proficient in classical learning' and in 'the modern languages'." Footnote by the Rev. T. Thomson, in his edition of Hogg's *Works* (London, 1865), vol. 2, p. 449. However, Jeffrey's review of *Anster Fair* follows immediately after his review of *The Queen's Wake*, and contains the words: "Mr Tennant is a kind of prodigy as well as Mr Hogg—and his book would be entitled to notice as a curiosity, even if its pretensions were much smaller than they are on the score of its literary merit" (*Edinburgh Review*, vol. 24 (1815), p. 174–5).

till he induced him to give up the bargain. It was in vain that I remonstrated, affirming that the work was my own, and I would give it to whom I pleased. I had no one to take my part, and I was browbeat out of it—Goldie alleging that I had no reason to complain, as he now entered precisely into Constable's terms, and had run all the risk of the former editions. I durst not say that he was going to break, and never pay me; so I was obliged to suffer the edition to be printed off in Goldie's name. This was exceeding ill done of him —nothing could be more cruel—and I was grieved that he did so, for I had a good opinion of him. The edition had not been lodged in his premises a week before he stopped payment, and yet, in that time, he had contrived to sell, or give away, more than one half of the copies; and thus all the little money that I had gained, which I was so proud of, and on which I depended for my subsistence, and the settling of some old farming debts that were pressing hard upon me, vanished from my grasp at once.

It was on the occasion of Mr. Blackwood being appointed one of the trustees upon the bankrupt estate that I was first introduced to him. I found him and the two Messrs. Bridges deeply interested in my case. I shall never forget their kindness and attention to my interests at that unfortunate period. I applied to Mr. Samuel Aitken, who was the head trustee, with fear and trembling, for I judged of him as a severe and strict man, who I knew would do justice to me, but I expected nothing farther. When I waited on him he looked at me with his grey stiff eye. "It is all over with me here," thought I. I never was more mistaken in my life; for no sooner had I stated my case than Samuel entered into my interests with his whole heart, and said, that provided he could save the creditors from losing any thing, which he was bound to do, he saw no right they had to make any thing by my edition. He then and there consigned over to me the whole of the remaining copies, 490 in number, charging me only with the expenses of printing, &c. These, to my agreeable astonishment, amounted only to two shillings and tenpence halfpenny per volume. The work sold at twelve shillings, so that a good reversion appeared to be mine. Mr. Blackwood sold the copies for me on commission, and ultimately paid me more than double of what I was to have received from Goldie. For this I was indebted to the consideration and kindness of the trustees.[55]

I had likewise, before this time, been introduced to most of the

[55] *I applied to Mr. Samuel Aitken . . . kindness of the trustees.*   Added in AT.

great literary characters in the metropolis, and lived with them on terms of intimacy, finding myself more and more a welcome guest at all their houses. However, I was careful not to abuse their indulgence; for, with the exception of a few intimate friends, I made myself exceedingly scarce. I was indebted for these introductions, in a great degree, to the Reverend Dr. Morehead,[56] one of the most amiable men I have ever known, and to two worthy ladies of the name of Lowes. I have written out, at great length, my opinion of all the characters of these literary gentlemen, with traits of their behaviour towards each other, principally from reports on which I could depend, and what I myself knew of their plans and parties; but this would fill a volume as large as the present work.

On the appearance of Mr. Wilson's "Isle of Palms,"[57] I was so greatly taken with many of his fanciful and visionary scenes, descriptive of bliss and woe, that it had a tendency to divest me occasionally of all worldly feelings. I reviewed this poem, as well as many others, in a Scottish Review then going on in Edinburgh, and was exceedingly anxious to meet with the author; but this I tried in vain, for the space of six months. All I could learn of him was, that he was a man from the mountains in Wales, or the west of England, with hair like eagles' feathers, and nails like birds' claws; a red beard, and an uncommon degree of wildness in his looks. Wilson was then utterly unknown in Edinburgh, except slightly to Mr. Walter Scott, who never introduces any one person to another, nor judges it of any avail. However, having no other shift left, I sat down and wrote him a note, telling him that I wished much to see him, and if he wanted to see me, he might come and dine with me at my lodgings in the Road of Gabriel, at four.[58] He accepted the invitation, and dined with Grieve and me; and I found him so much a man according to my own heart, that for many years we were seldom twenty-four hours asunder, when in town. I afterwards went and visited him, staying with him a month at his seat in Westmoreland,[59] where we

56 The Rev. Robert Morehead, D.D. (1777-1842) was one of the ministers of St Paul's Episcopal Chapel, York Place, Edinburgh. He published a number of poems, and corresponded with Scott, Byron and others. Hogg mentions Morehead again later in the *Memoir*.

57 John Wilson (1785-1854), "Christopher North", author of the *Noctes Ambrosianae*. The *Isle of Palms* was published in 1812.

58 21 has " . . . at four; and if not, he might stay at home."

59 Elleray, overlooking Windermere, where Wilson associated with Wordsworth, Southey, Coleridge and De Quincey.

had some curious doings among the gentlemen and poets of the lakes. It is a pity I have not room here to give a description of all these scenes, being obliged, according to my plan, to return to a subject far less interesting, namely, my own literary progress.

The "Queen's Wake" being now consigned to Messrs. Murray and Blackwood, I fairly left it to its fate; and they published a fourth edition, which was in fact not a new edition, but only the remainder of Goldie's third; so that I gained an edition in the eyes of the world, although not in the weight of my purse, to which this edition in reality made no *addition*. It has, however, been a good work to me, and has certainly been read and admired much above what its merits warrant. My own opinion of it is, that it is a very imperfect and unequal production; and if it were not for three of the ballads, which are rather of a redeeming quality, some of the rest are little better than trash. But, somehow or other, the plan proved extremely happy; and though it was contrived solely for the purpose of stringing my miscellaneous ballads into a regular poem, happened to have a good effect, from keeping always up a double interest, both in the incidents of each tale, and in the success of the singer in the contest for the prize harp. The intermediate poetry between the ballads is all likewise middling good.[60]

The same year in which I wrote the two musical dramas, I also wrote a tragedy, which was called "The Hunting of Badlewe;" but of this Goldie only printed a few copies, to see how the public relished it. It was not favourably received;—but more of this hereafter.

Although it should rather have been mentioned at a period subsequent to this, I may take notice here, that the *fifth edition* of the "Queen's Wake," in royal octavo, with plates, was a plan concocted by Mr. Blackwood to bring me in a little money. He was assisted in this undertaking by Charles Sharpe, Esq.,[61] Mr. Walter Scott, and several other friends; but most of all by the indefatigable Mr. David Bridges, junior, a man that often effects more in one day than many others can do in six, and who is, in fact, a greater prodigy than any self-taught painter or poet in the kingdom.

The only other anecdote which I have recorded in my Diary

---

[60] Hogg's two outstanding poems, "Kilmeny" and "The Witch of Fife", are ballads from *The Queen's Wake*. The linking narrative concerns a poetic contest held in honour of Mary Queen of Scots on her return from France.

[61] Charles Kirkpatrick Sharpe (1781?–1851), the antiquary and life-long friend of Scott.

relating to this poem is one about the dedication. As it related to the amusements of a young queen, I thought I could dedicate it to no one so appropriately as to her royal and beautiful descendant, the Princess Charlotte; which I did. By the advice of some friends, I got a large paper copy bound up in an elegant antique style, which cost three guineas, and sent it as a present to her Royal Highness, directing it to the care of Dr. Fisher, bishop of Salisbury, and requesting him to present it to his royal pupil. His lordship was neither at the pains to acknowledge the receipt of the work or of my letter, nor, I dare say, to deliver it as directed. The dedication I have never had the heart to cancel, even now when she is no more, and I have let the original date remain.

During all this time I generally went on a tour into the Highlands every summer, and always made a point of tarrying some time at Kinnaird House in Athol,[62] the seat of Chalmers Izett, Esq., whose lady had taken an early interest in my fortunes, which no circumstance has ever abated. I depended much on her advice and good taste; and had I attended more to her friendly remonstrances, it would have been much better for me. In the summer of 1814, having been seized with a severe cold while there, it was arranged that I should reside at Kinnaird House two or three weeks; and as Mrs. Izett insisted that I should not remain idle, she conducted me up stairs one morning, and introduced me into a little study, furnished with books and writing materials. "Now," said she, "I do not wish you to curtail your fishing hours, since you seem to delight so much in it, but whenever you have a spare hour, either evening or morning, you can retire to this place, either to read or write, as the humour suits you."—"Since you will set me down to write," said I, "you must choose a subject for me, for I have nothing in hand, and have thought of nothing."—"How can you be at a loss for a subject," returned she, "and that majestic river rolling beneath your eyes?" —"Well," said I, "though I consider myself exquisite at descriptions of nature, and mountain-scenery in particular, yet I am afraid that a poem wholly descriptive will prove dull and heavy."—"You may make it the shorter," said she; "only write something to prevent your mind from rusting."

Upon this I determined immediately to write a poem descriptive

[62] This mansion, beautifully situated on ground overlooking the Tay, was tenanted during 1823-4 by the Bullers, whose tutor, Thomas Carlyle (1795-1881), here wrote most of his *Life of Schiller* and the first part of his translation of *Wilhelm Meister*.

D

of the river Tay, and after spending about two hours considering in what verse I should write it, I fixed on the stanza of Spenser. "That is the finest verse in the world," said I to myself; "it rolls off with such majesty and grandeur. What an effect it will have in the description of mountains, cataracts, and storms!"

I had also another motive for adopting it. I was fond of the Spenserian measure; but there was something in the best models that always offended my ear. It was owing to this. I thought it so formed, that every verse ought to be a structure of itself, resembling an arch, of which the two meeting rhymes in the middle should represent the key-stone, and on these all the strength and flow of the verse should rest. On beginning this poem, therefore, I had the vanity to believe that I was going to give the world a new specimen of this stanza in its proper harmony. It was under these feelings that my poem of "Mador of the Moor" was begun, and in a very short time completed: but I left out to the extent of one whole book of the descriptive part.[63] There is no doubt whatever that my highest and most fortunate efforts in rhyme are contained in some of the descriptions of nature in that poem, and in the "Ode to Superstition" in the same measure.[64]

In the same year, and immediately on finishing the above poem, I conceived a plan for writing a volume of romantic poems, to be entitled "Midsummer Night Dreams," and am sorry to this day that a friendly advice prevented me from accomplishing my design, for of all other subjects, there were none that suited the turn of my thoughts so well.

The first of these dreams that I wrote was "Connel of Dee," now published in the "Winter Evening Tales," and the second was "The Pilgrims of the Sun." It happened that a gentleman, Mr. James Park of Greenock, on whose literary taste I had great reliance, came to Edinburgh for a few weeks about this time; and, as we had been intimate acquaintances and correspondents for a number of years, I gave him a perusal of all my recent pieces in manuscript. His approbation of the "Pilgrims of the Sun" was so decided, and so unqualified, that he prevailed upon me to give up my design of the Midsummer Night Dreams, and also that of publishing Mador, and to publish the former poem as an entire work by itself. This advice

[63] *Mador of the Moor* was published by Blackwood in 1816. Like Scott's *Lady of the Lake*, *Mador* tells of the adventures of a king wandering in disguise.

[64] "Superstition" was first published in *Pilgrims of the Sun* (1815).

of my inestimable and regretted friend, though given in sincerity of heart, I am convinced was wrong; but I had faith in every one that commended any of my works, and laughed at those who did otherwise, thinking, and asserting, that they had not sufficient discernment. Among other wild and visionary subjects, the "Pilgrims of the Sun" would have done very well, and might at least have been judged one of the best; but, as an entire poem by itself, it bears an impress of extravagance, and affords no relief from the story of a visionary existence. After my literary blunders and miscarriages are a few months old, I can view them with as much indifference, and laugh at them as heartily, as any of my neighbours. I have often felt, that Mary Lee reminded me of a beautiful country girl turned into an assembly in dishabille, "half-naked, for a warld's wonder," whose beauties might be gazed at, but were sure to be derided.[65]

There were some circumstances attending the publication of this poem which show the doings and the honour of the bookselling profession in a peculiar light. I called on my old friend, Mr. Constable, from whom I was very loath to part, and told him my design and views in publishing the poem. He received me with his usual kindness, and seemed to encourage the plan: but, in the mean time, said he was busy, and that if I would call again on Saturday, he would have time to think of it, and give me an answer. With the solicitude of a poor author, I was punctual to my hour on Saturday, and found Mr. Constable sitting at his confined desk up stairs, and alone, which was a rare incident. He saluted me, held out his hand without lifting his eyes from the paper, and then, resuming his pen, continued writing. I read the backs of some of the books on his shelves, and then spoke of my new poem; but he would not deign to lift his eyes, or regard me. I tried to bring on a conversation by talking of the Edinburgh Review;[66] but all to no purpose. "Now, the devil confound the fellow," thought I to myself, "he will sit there scribbling till we are interrupted by some one coming to talk to him of business, and then I shall lose my opportunity—perhaps it is what he wants! Hang[67] him, if I thought he were not wanting my book, I should be

[65] *Pilgrims of the Sun* was published by Blackwood in 1815. Like the heroine of "Kilmeny", Mary Lee in *Pilgrims* is a beautiful virgin who is taken to heaven because of her perfect purity. *Pilgrims* is much longer and more elaborate than "Kilmeny", and fails to repeat the earlier poem's success.

[66] Published by Constable.

[67] *Hang* 21 "D——m"

as saucy as he is!" At length he turned his back to the window, with his face to me, and addressed me in a long set speech, a thing I never heard him do before. It had a great deal of speciousness in it; but with regard to its purport, I leave the world to judge. I pledge myself, that in this short Sketch of my Literary Life, as well as in the extended memoir, should that ever appear, to relate nothing but the downright truth. If any should feel that they have done or said wrong, I cannot help it.

"By G——, Hogg, you are a very extraordinary fellow!" said he —"you are a man of very great genius, sir! I don't know if ever there was such another man born!" I looked down, and brushed my hat with my elbow; for what could any man answer to such an address? "Nay, it is all true, sir; I do not jest a word—I never knew such a genius in my life. I am told that, since the publication of the "Queen's Wake" last year, you have three new poems, all as long, and greatly superior to that, ready for publication. By G——, sir, you will write Scott, and Byron, and every one of them, off the field."

"Let us alane o' your gibes, Maister Constable," said I, "and tell me at ance what ye 're gaun to say about yon."

"I have been thinking seriously about your proposal, Hogg," said he; "and though you are the very sort of man whom I wish to encourage, yet I do not think the work would be best in my hands. I am so deeply engaged, my dear sir, in large and ponderous works, that a small light work has no good chance in my hands at all. For the sake of the authors, I have often taken such works in hand—among others, your friend Mr. Paterson's[68]—and have been grieved that I had it not in my power to pay that minute attention to them, individually, that I wished to have done. The thing is impossible! And then the authors come fretting to me; nor will they believe that another bookseller can do much more for such works than I can. There is my friend, Mr. Miller, for instance—he has sold three times as many of *Discipline* as perhaps I could have done."—"No, no," said I, "I'll deal none with Mr. Miller: if you are not for the work yourself, I will find out one who will take it."—"I made the proposal in friendship," said he: "if you give the work to Miller I shall do all for it the same as if it were my own. I will publish it in all my catalogues, and in all my reviews and magazines, and I will send it abroad with all these to my agents in the country. I will be

[68] *The Legend of Iona, with Other Poems*, by Walter Paterson, was published by Constable in 1814.

security for the price of it, should you and he deal; so that, in trans-
ferring it to Miller in place of me, you only secure for it two interests
in place of one."

This was all so unobjectionable, that I could say nothing in opposition to it; so we agreed on the price at one word, which was, I
think, to be eighty-six[69] pounds for liberty to print one thousand
copies. Mr. Miller was sent for, who complied with every thing as
implicitly as if he had been Mr. Constable's clerk, and without
making a single observation. The bargain was fairly made out and
concluded; the manuscript was put into Mr. Miller's hands, and I
left Edinburgh, leaving him a written direction how to forward the
proofs. Week passed after week, and no proofs arrived. I grew impatient, it having been stipulated that the work was to be published
in two months, and wrote to Mr. Miller; but I received no answer.
I then wrote to a friend to inquire the reason. He waited on Mr.
Miller, he said, but received no satisfactory answer: "the truth of
the matter," added he, "is this: Mr. Miller, I am privately informed,
sent out your MS. among his blue-stockings for their verdict. They
have condemned the poem as extravagant nonsense Mr Miller has
rued his bargain, and will never publish the poem, unless he is sued
at law." How far this information was correct I had no means of
discovering; but it vexed me exceedingly, as I had mentioned the
transaction to all my friends, and how much I was pleased at the
connexion. However, I waited patiently for two months, the time
when it ought to have been published, and then I wrote Mr. Miller
a note, desiring him to put my work forthwith to the press, the time
being now elapsed; or, otherwise, to return me the manuscript. Mr.
Miller returned me the poem with a polite note, as if no bargain had
existed, and I thought it beneath me ever to mention the circumstance again, either to him or Mr. Constable.[70] As I never understood the real secret of this transaction, neither do I know whom to
blame. Mr. Miller seemed all along to be acting on the ground of

[69] *eighty-six* 21 "eighty".

[70] In a letter to Byron, dated 11 October 1814, Hogg writes: "I told you I had sold
an edition of a new poem to Constable and Miller;—on my return to town, after an
absence of 3 weeks, by which time it was to have been published, I found it in the same
state in which I had left it, and the MS. taken out of the press and passing through all
the notable *blues*. I went to the shop in a tremendous rage, threatened Miller with a
prosecution, and took the MS. out of his hands. So that, If Murray and I do not agree,
I am in a fine scrape." See A. L. Strout, *The Life and Letters of James Hogg* (1946),
p. 85-6. John Murray of Albemarle Street (1778-1843) was Byron's publisher.

some secret arrangement with his neighbour, and it was perhaps by an arrangement of the same kind that the poem was given up. But I only relate what I know.

Some time after this Mr. Blackwood introduced me to Mr. John Murray, the London bookseller, with whom I was quite delighted; and one night, after supping with him in Albany Street, I mentioned the transaction with Mr. Miller. He said Mr. Constable was to blame; for, as matters stood, he ought to have seen the bargain implemented; but, at all events, it should be no loss to me, for he was willing to take the poem according to Mr. Miller's bargain. There was nothing more said; we at once agreed, and exchanged letters on it; the work was put to press, and soon finished. But, alas! for my unfortunate Pilgrim! The running copy was sent up to Mr. Murray in London; and that gentleman, finding his critical friends of the same opinion with Mr. Miller's blue-stockings, would not allow his name to go to the work. It was in vain that Mr. Blackwood urged that it was a work of genius, however faulty, and that it would be an honour for any bookseller to have his name to it. Mr. Murray had been informed, by those on whose judgment he could rely, that it was the most wretched poem that ever was written.

Mr. Blackwood felt a delicacy in telling me this, and got a few friends to inform me of it in as delicate a way as possible. I could not, however, conceal my feelings, and maintained that the poem was a good one. Mr. Grieve checked me, by saying it was impossible that I could be a better judge than both the literary people of Scotland and England—that they could have no interest in condemning the poem; and after what had happened, it was vain to augur any good of it. I said it would be long ere any of those persons who had condemned it could write one like it; and I was obliged to please myself with this fancy, and put up with the affront.

The poem came out, and was rather well received. I never met with any person, who really had read it, that did not like the piece; the reviewers praised it; and the Eclectic,[71] in particular, gave it the highest commendation I ever saw bestowed on a work of genius. It was reprinted in two different towns in America, and ten thousand copies of it sold in that country.[72] Mr. Murray very honourably paid

[71] The *Eclectic Review* was published in London from 1805 to 1868, and has been described as "a sectarian religious organ of the Dissenters".

[72] There is in the National Library of Scotland a copy of an edition of *Pilgrims* published in Philadelphia in 1815. Hogg no doubt exaggerates his American sales.

me the price agreed on three months before it was due; but the work sold heavily here, and neither my booksellers nor I have proposed a second edition. The trade were all, except Mr. Blackwood, set against it, in defence of their own good taste. It is indeed a faulty poem, but I think no shame of it; neither, I trust, will any of my friends when I am no more.

My next literary adventure was the most extravagant of any. I took it into my head that I would collect a poem from every living author in Britain, and publish them in a neat and elegant volume, by which I calculated I might make my fortune. I either applied personally, or by letter, to Southey, Wilson, Wordsworth, Lloyd, Morehead, Pringle, Paterson,[73] and several others; all of whom sent me very ingenious and beautiful poems. Wordsworth afterwards reclaimed his; and although Lord Byron and Rogers both promised, neither of them ever performed. I believe they intended it, but some other concerns of deeper moment interfered. In one of Lord Byron's letters he told me he was busy inditing a poem for me, and assured me that "he would appear in my work in his best breeks." That poem was "Lara," and who it was that influenced him to detain it from me, I do not know. I have heard a report of one; but the deed was so ungenerous, I cannot believe it.

I may here mention, by way of advertising, that I have lost all Lord Byron's letters to me, on which I put a very high value;[74] and which I know to have been stolen from me by some one or other of my tourist visitors, for I was so proud of these letters, that I would always be showing them to every body. It was exceedingly unkind, particularly as they never can be of use to any other person, for they have been so often and so eagerly read by many of my friends, that any single sentence out of any one of them could easily be detected. I had five letters of his of two sheets each, and one of three. They were indeed queer *harumscarum letters*, about women, and poetry, mountains, and authors, and blue-stockings; and what he sat down to write about was generally put in the postscript. They were all, however, extremely kind, save one, which was rather a satirical, bitter letter. I had been quizzing him about his approaching marriage, and

[73] Wilson, Lloyd, Morehead, Pringle and Paterson are all mentioned elsewhere in the footnotes.

[74] One letter by Byron to Hogg is printed in R. E. Prothero's edition of Byron's *Letters and Journals* (London, 1898–1901), vol. 3, p. 268–70. Prothero in a footnote quotes Hogg's friend D. M. Moir (1798–1851), who writes of two other letters by Byron to Hogg. Three letters by Hogg to Byron are also printed by Prothero (vol. 3, p. 392–6.)

assuring him that he was going to get himself into a confounded scrape. I wished she might prove both a good *mill* and a *bank* to him; but I much doubted they would not be such as he was calculating on. I think he felt that I was using too much freedom with him.

The last letter that I received from him was shortly after the birth of his daughter Ada. In it he breathed the most tender affection both for the mother and child. Good Heaven! how I was astounded by the news that soon followed that!—Peace be to his manes! He was a great man; and I do not think that one on earth appreciated his gigantic genius so highly as I did. He sent me previous to that period all his poems as they were printed.

But to return to my publication:[75] Mr. Walter Scott absolutely refused to furnish me with even one verse, which I took exceedingly ill, as it frustrated my whole plan. What occasioned it I do not know, as I accounted myself certain of his support from the beginning, and had never asked any thing of him in all my life that he refused. It was in vain that I represented that I had done as much for him, and would do ten times more if he required it. He remained firm in his denial, which I thought very hard; so I left him in high dudgeon, sent him a very abusive letter, and would not speak to him again for many a day. I could not even endure to see him at a distance, I felt so degraded by the refusal; and I was, at that time, more disgusted with all mankind than I had ever been before, or have ever been since.[76]

I began, with a heavy heart, to look over the pieces I had received, and lost all hope of the success of my project. They were, indeed, all very well; but I did not see that they possessed such merit as could give celebrity to any work; and after considering them well, I fancied that I could write a better poem than any that had been sent or would be sent to me, and this so completely in the style of each poet, that it should not be known but for his own production. It was this conceit that suggested to me the idea of "The Poetic Mirror, or Living Bards of Britain." I set to work with great glee, as the fancy had struck me, and in a few days I finished my imitations of Wordsworth and Lord Byron. Like a fool, I admired the latter poem most, and contrived to get a large literary party together, on

[75] *In one of Lord Byron's letters he told me . . . my publication*: Added in AT.

[76] Hogg's account of his quarrel with Scott and his account of the genesis of *The Poetic Mirror* are discussed in the Commentary. There is evidence which suggests that the *Memoir* may be misleading here.

pretence, as I said, of giving them a literary treat. I had got the
poem transcribed, and gave it to Mr. Ballantyne to read, who did
it ample justice. Indeed, he read it with extraordinary effect; so
much so, that I was astonished at the poem myself, and before it
was half done all pronounced it Byron's. Every one was deceived,
except Mr. Ballantyne, who was not to be imposed on in that way;
but he kept the secret until we got to the bridge, and then he told
me his mind.

The "Poetic Mirror"[77] was completely an off-hand production. I
wrote it all in three weeks, except a very small proportion; and in
less than three months it was submitted to the public. The second
poem in the volume, namely, the Epistle to R—— S——, the most
beautiful and ingenious piece in the work, is not mine. It was written
by Mr. Thomas Pringle,[78] and was not meant as an imitation of Mr.
Scott's manner at all. There is likewise another small secret connected with that work, which I am not yet at liberty to unfold, but
which the ingenious may perhaps discover. The first edition was
sold in six weeks, and another of seven hundred and fifty copies has
since been sold. I do not set any particular value on any poem in
the work by myself, except "The Gude Greye Katte," which was
written as a caricature of "The Pilgrims of the Sun," the "Witch of
Fife," and some others of my fairy ballads. It is greatly superior to
any of them. I have also been told, that in England, one of the
imitations of Wordsworth's Excursion has been deemed excellent.

The year following I published two volumes of Tragedies: to
these I affixed the title of "Dramatic Tales, by the Author of the
Poetic Mirror." I forgot, however, to mention, that the Poetic
Mirror was published anonymously, and I was led to think that, had
the imitations of Wordsworth been less a caricature, the work might
have passed, for a season at least, as the genuine productions of the
authors themselves, whose names were prefixed to the several poems.
I was strongly urged by some friends, previous to the publication
of these plays, to try "Sir Anthony Moore" on the stage; and once,
at the suggestions of Sir Walter Scott, I consented to submit it to
the players, through Mr. Ballantyne. But, by a trivial accident, the

---

[77] *The Poetic Mirror* contains several brilliant parodies of the poetry of Hogg's contemporaries, and is one of his more notable achievements in verse. It was published by
Longman and John Ballantyne in 1816.

[78] Thomas Pringle (1789–1834), the Scottish poet, gained Scott's friendship as a
result of his contribution to *The Poetic Mirror*.

matter was delayed till I got time to consider of it; and then I shrunk from the idea of intrusting my character as a poet in the hands of every bungling and absurd actor, who, if dissatisfied with his part, had the power of raising as much disapprobation as might damn the whole piece. Consequently, my first attempts in the drama have never been offered for representation. "Sir Anthony Moore" is the least original, and the least poetical piece of the whole, and I trust it will never be acted while I live; but, if at any period it should be brought forward, and one able performer appear in the character of Old Cecil, and another in that of Caroline, I may venture my credit and judgment, as an author, that it will prove successful. The pastoral drama of "All-Hallow Eve" was written at the suggestion of the Reverend Robert Morehead. "The Profligate Princes" is a modification of my first play, "The Hunting of Badlewe," printed by Goldie; and the fragment of "The Haunted Glen" was written off-hand, to make the second volume of an equal extent with the first.[79]

The small degree of interest that these dramas excited in the world finished my dramatic and poetical career. I had adopted a resolution of writing a drama every year as long as I lived, hoping to make myself perfect by degrees, as a man does in his calling, by serving an apprenticeship; but the failure of those to excite notice fully convinced me, that either this was not the age to appreciate the qualities of dramatic composition, or that I was not possessed of the talents fitting me for such an undertaking: and so I gave up the ambitious design.

Before this period, all the poems that I had published had been begun and written by chance and at random, without any previous design. I had at that time commenced an epic poem on a regular plan, and I finished two books of it, pluming myself that it was to prove my greatest work. But, seeing that the poetical part of these dramas excited no interest in the public, I felt conscious that no poetry I should ever be able to write would do so; or, if it did, the success would hinge upon some casualty, on which it did not behove me to rely. So, from that day to this, save now and then an idle song to beguile a leisure hour, I determined to write no more poetry.

Several years subsequent to this, at the earnest intreaties of some literary friends, I once more set to work and finished this poem,

[79] Hogg's *Dramatic Tales* were published by Longman and John Ballantyne in two volumes in 1817. *The Hunting of Badlewe* had been published by Goldie in 1814.

which I entitled "Queen Hynde,"[80] in a time shorter than any person would believe. I submitted it first to Sir Walter Scott, who gave it his approbation in the most unqualified terms; so the work was put to press with every prospect of high success. I sold an edition of one thousand copies to Longman and Co.; but Mr. Blackwood, who had been chiefly instrumental in urging me to finish the poem, claimed the half of the edition, and got it. But it proved to him like the Highlandman's character—"he would have peen as petter without it." That malicious *deevil*, Jerdan,[81] first took it up and damned it with faint praise. The rest of the reviewers followed in his wake, so that, in short, the work sold heavily and proved rather a failure.

It is said the multitude never are wrong, but, in this instance, I must take Mr. Wordsworth's plan, and maintain that they *were* wrong. I need not say how grievously I was disappointed, as what unsuccessful candidate for immortal fame is not? But it would have been well could I have refrained from exposing myself. I was invited to a public dinner given by a great number of young friends, a sort of worshippers of mine (for I have a number of those in Scotland) It was to congratulate me on my new work, and drink success to it. The president made a speech, in which, after some laudatory remarks on the new poem, he boldly and broadly asserted that it was much inferior to their beloved "Queen's Wake." I was indignantly wroth, denying his assertion both in principle and position, and maintained not only that it was infinitely superior to the "Queen's Wake," but I offered to bet the price of the edition with any or all of them that it was the best epic poem that ever had been produced in Scotland. None of them would take the bet, but as few backed me. I will however stake my credit on "Queen Hynde." It was unfortunate that the plot should have been laid in an age so early that we have no interest in it.[82]

From the time I gave up "The Spy" I had been planning with my friends to commence the publication of a Magazine on a new plan; but, for several years, we only conversed about the utility of such a work, without doing any thing farther. At length, among

[80] Published in 1825.

[81] William Jerdan (1782–1862), a native of Kelso, was a journalist in London from 1801. He edited the *Literary Gazette* 1817–50.

[82] *Several years subsequent to this ... interest in it.* Added in AT. *Queen Hynde* deals with an invasion of Scotland by the Norwegians in the time of St Columba.

others, I chanced to mention it to Mr. Thomas Pringle; when I found that he and his friends had a plan in contemplation of the same kind. We agreed to join our efforts, and try to set it a-going; but, as I declined the editorship on account of residing mostly on my farm at a distance from town, it became a puzzling question who was the best qualified among our friends for that undertaking. We at length fixed on Mr. Gray as the fittest person for a principal department, and I went and mentioned the plan to Mr. Blackwood, who, to my astonishment, I found had likewise long been cherishing a plan of the same kind. He said he knew nothing about Pringle, and always had his eye on me as a principal assistant; but he would not begin the undertaking until he saw he could do it with effect. Finding him, however, disposed to encourage such a work, Pringle, at my suggestion, made out a plan in writing, with a list of his supporters, and sent it in a letter to me. I inclosed it in another, and sent it to Mr. Blackwood; and not long after that period Pringle and he came to an arrangement about commencing the work, while I was in the country. Thus I had the honour of being the beginner, and almost sole instigator of that celebrated work, "Blackwood's Magazine;" but from the time I heard that Pringle had taken in Cleghorn as a partner I declined all connexion with it, farther than as an occasional contributor.[83] I told him the connexion would not likely last for a year, and insisted that he should break it at once; but to this proposal he would in nowise listen. As I had predicted, so it fell out, and much sooner than might have been expected. In the fourth month after the commencement of that work, I received a letter from Mr. Blackwood, soliciting my return to Edinburgh; and when I arrived there, I found that he and his two redoubted editors had gone to loggerheads, and instead of arguing the matter face to face, they were corresponding together at the rate of about a sheet an hour. Viewing this as a ridiculous mode of proceeding, I brought about two meetings between Mr. Blackwood and Mr. Pringle, and endeavoured all that I could to bring them to a right understanding about the matter. A reconciliation was effected at that time, and I returned again into the country. Soon, however, I heard that the

[83] *Blackwood's Magazine* started life in April 1817 as the *Edinburgh Monthly Magazine*, edited by Thomas Pringle (1789–1834), who had contributed to Hogg's *Poetic Mirror* (1816), and by James Cleghorn (1778–1838), an actuary and farmer. As a result of the quarrel between Blackwood and his editors the journal changed its name to *Blackwood's Magazine*. The "Chaldee Manuscript" appeared in the first number of the renamed journal, in September 1817.

flames of controversy, and proud opposition, had broken out between the parties with greater fury than ever; and, shortly after, that they had finally separated, and the two champions gone over and enlisted under the banners of Mr. Constable, having left Mr. Blackwood to shift for himself, and carried over, as they pretended, their right to the Magazine, with all their subscribers and contributors, to the other side.

I received letters from both parties. I loved Pringle, and would gladly have assisted him had it been in my power; but, after balancing fairly the two sides, I thought Mr. Blackwood more sinned against than sinning, and that the two editors had been endeavouring to bind him to a plan which could not possibly succeed; so, on considering his disinterested friendship for me, manifested in several strong instances, I stuck to him, expecting excellent sport in the various exertions and manAuvres of the two parties for the superiority.

I know not what wicked genius put it into my head, but it was then, in an evil hour, when I had determined on the side I was to espouse, that I wrote the "Chaldee Manuscript," and transmitted it to Mr. Blackwood from Yarrow. On first reading it, he never thought of publishing it; but some of the rascals to whom he showed it, after laughing at it, by their own accounts till they were sick, persuaded him, nay almost forced him, to insert it; for some of them went so far as to tell him, that if he did not admit that inimitable article, they would never speak to him again so long as they lived. Needless however it is now to deny, that they interlarded it with a good deal of deevilry of their own, which I had never thought of; and one who had a principal hand in these alterations has never yet been named as an aggressor.[84]

Certain of my literary associates call me *The Chaldee Shepherd*, and pretend to sneer at my assumption of being the author of that celebrated article. Certes they have long ago persuaded the country that I was not. Luckily, however, I have preserved the original proof slips and three of Mr. Blackwood's letters relating to the article.

[84] Lockhart and Wilson, who became the chief supporters of *Blackwood's Magazine* after the departure of Cleghorn and Pringle, took a leading part in the revision of "The Chaldee Manuscript". The scandal caused by the publication of the "Manuscript" greatly increased *Blackwood's* readership. The Blackwood Papers, now in the National Library of Scotland, contain material relating to the "Chaldee Manuscript", including Hogg's original draft. This material is discussed in "James Hogg's 'Chaldee Manuscript' ", by A. L. Strout, *PMLA*, vol. 65 (1950), p. 695–718. Hogg, writing from memory in London, overstates the proportion of the published text which was by him, but his account is otherwise accurate.

These proofs show exactly what part was mine, which, if I remember aright (for I write this in London), consists of the first two chapters, part of the third, and part of the last. The rest was said to have been made up conjointly in full divan. I do not know, but I always suspected Lockhart of a heavy responsibility there.[85]

I declare I never once dreamed of giving anybody offence by that droll article, nor did I ever think of keeping it a secret either from Mr. Constable or Mr. Pringle: so far from that, I am sure, had I been in town, I would have shown the manuscript to the latter before publication. I meant it as a sly history of the transaction, and the great literary battle that was to be fought. All that I expected was a little retaliation of the same kind in the opposing magazine; and when I received letter after letter, informing me what a dreadful flame it had raised in Edinburgh, I could not be brought to believe that it was not a joke. I am not certain but that I confessed the matter to Mr. George Thomson, in the course of our correspondence, before I was aware of its importance. No one ever suspected me as the author. When I came to town, every one made his remarks, and pronounced his anathemas upon it, without any reserve, in my hearing, which afforded me much amusement. Still I could not help viewing the whole as a farce, or something unreal and deceptive; and I am sure I never laughed so much in my life as at the rage in which I found so many people.

So little had I intended giving offence by what appeared in the Magazine, that I had written out a long continuation of the manuscript, which I have by me to this day, in which I go over the painters, poets, lawyers, booksellers, magistrates, and ministers of Edinburgh, all in the same style; and with reference to the first part that was published, I might say of the latter as king Rehoboam said to the elders of Israel, "My little finger was thicker than my father's loins." It took all the energy of Mr. Wilson and his friends, and some sharp remonstrances from Sir Walter Scott, as well as a great deal of controversy and battling with Mr. Grieve, to prevent me from publishing the whole work as a large pamphlet, and putting my name to it.

That same year I published "The Brownie of Bodsbeck," and other Tales, in two volumes. I suffered unjustly in the eyes of the world with regard to that tale, which was looked on as an imitation of the tale of "Old Mortality," and a counterpart to that; whereas

[85] *Certain of my . . . responsibility there.*   Added in AT.

it was written long ere the tale of "Old Mortality" was heard of, and I well remember my chagrin on finding the ground, which I thought clear, pre-occupied before I could appear publicly on it, and that by such a redoubted champion. It was wholly owing to Mr. Blackwood that this tale was not published a year sooner, which would effectually have freed me from the stigma of being an imitator, and brought in the author of the "Tales of My Landlord" as an imitator of me. That was the only ill turn that ever Mr. Blackwood did me; and it ought to be a warning to authors never to intrust booksellers with their manuscripts.

I mentioned to Mr. Blackwood that I had two tales I wished to publish, and at his request I gave him a reading of the manuscript. One of them was "The Brownie," which, I believe, was not quite finished.[86] He approved of it, but with "The Bridal of Polmood" he would have nothing to do. Of course, my manuscripts were returned, and I had nothing else for it but to retire to the country, and there begin and write two other tales in place of the one rejected. "The Bridal of Polmood," however, was published from the same copy, and without the alteration of a word, and has been acknowledged by all who have read it as the most finished and best written tale that I ever produced. Mr. Blackwood himself must be sensible of this fact, and also, that in preventing its being published along with "The Brownie of Bodsbeck," he did an injury both to himself and me. As a farther proof how little booksellers are to be trusted, he likewise wished to prevent the insertion of "The Wool-Gatherer," which has been a universal favourite; but I know the source from whence it proceeded. I would never object trusting a bookseller, were he a man of any taste; for, unless he wishes to reject an author

[86] *The Brownie of Bodsbeck* was published in 1818, *Old Mortality* in December 1816. Two letters of January 1818 (one from Blackwood to William Laidlaw, and the other from Hogg to Blackwood) indicate that *The Brownie* was not completed at that date. Both letters are quoted in Strout, *Life and Letters of James Hogg* (1946), p. 146. Robert Carruthers in the *Abbotsford Notanda* printed in Robert Chambers's *Life of Sir Walter Scott* (1871) asks how Blackwood could go to press in 1816 with a story unfinished in January 1818, and concludes that Hogg's "accusation is altogether a myth". He appears to have overlooked Hogg's statement in the *Memoir* that *The Brownie* "was not quite finished" when it was first sent to Blackwood. Strout has pointed out (p. 147) that in a letter to *The Scotsman* of 17 May 1818 Hogg stated that "the Brownie was written long before Old Mortality but I could not get the Booksellers to publish it". *The Woolgatherer* was published with *The Hunt of Eildon* in the second volume of *The Brownie*, while *The Bridal of Polmood* was published in Hogg's *Winter Evening Tales* (Edinburgh, Oliver and Boyd, 1820). Hogg also discusses *The Brownie* and *Old Mortality* in the *Familiar Anecdotes*, p. 105-7.

altogether, he can have no interest in asserting what he does not think. But the plague is, they *never read works themselves*, but give them to their minions, with whom there never fails to lurk a literary jealousy; and whose suggestions may uniformly be regarded as any thing but the truth. For my own part, I know that I have always been looked on by the learned part of the community as an intruder in the paths of literature, and every opprobrium has been thrown on me from that quarter. The truth is, that I am so. The walks of learning are occupied by a powerful aristocracy, who deem that province their own peculiar right; else, what would avail all their dear-bought collegiate honours and degrees? No wonder that they should view an intruder, from the humble and despised ranks of the community, with a jealous and indignant eye, and impede his progress by every means in their power.

I was unlucky therefore in the publication of my first novel, and what impeded me still farther, was the publication of "Old Mortality;" for, having made the redoubted Burley the hero of my tale, I was obliged to go over it again, and alter all the traits in the character of the principal personage, substituting John Brown of Caldwell for John Balfour of Burley, greatly to the detriment of my story. I tried also to take out Clavers, but I found this impossible. A better instance could not be given of the good luck attached to one person, and the bad luck which attended the efforts of another.

I observe that in the extended MS. I had detailed all the proceedings of a club, the most ridiculous perhaps that ever was established in any city, and, owing to some particular circumstances, I cannot refrain from mentioning them here. This club was established one night, in a frolic, at a jovial dinner party, in the house of a young lawyer, now of some celebrity at the bar, and was christened *The Right and Wrong Club*. The chief principle of the club was, that whatever any of its members should assert, the whole were bound to support the same, whether *right or wrong*. We were so delighted with the novelty of the idea, that we agreed to meet the next day at Oman's Hotel, and celebrate its anniversary. We were dull and heavy when we met, but did not part so. We dined at five, and separated at two in the morning, before which time the club had risen greatly in our estimation; so we agreed to meet next day, and every successive day for five or six weeks, and during all that time our hours of sitting continued the same. No constitutions on earth could stand this. Had our meetings been restricted to once a month, or even once a week, the club might have continued to this day, and would have been a source of much pleasure and entertainment to the members; but to meet daily was out of the question. The result was, that several of the members got quite deranged, and I drank myself into an inflammatory fever. The madness of the members proved no bar to the hilarity of the society; on the contrary it seemed to add a great deal of zest to it, as a thing quite in character. An inflammatory fever, however, sounded rather strange in the ears of the joyous group, and threw a damp on their spirits. They continued their meetings for some days longer, and regularly sent a deputation at five o'clock to inquire after my health, and I was sometimes favoured with a call from one or more of the members, between two and three in the morning, when they separated. The mornings after such visits I was almost sure to have to provide new knockers and bell-handles for all the people on the stair. Finding, however, that I still grew worse, they had the generosity to discontinue their sittings, and to declare that they would not meet again until their poet was able to join them; and if that should never happen, they would never meet again. This motion (which was made by a newly-initiated member, Mr. John Ballantyne,) was hailed with shouts of approbation, and from that hour to this *The Right and Wrong Club* never more met. It was high time that it should have been given up, for one term at least. It proved a dear club to me. I was three weeks confined to my bed, and if it had not been for Dr. Saunders, I believe I should have died. Its effect turned out better with regard to several of the other members, as it produced a number of happy marriages. During the period of high-excitation, the lads wrote flaming love-letters to young ladies of their acquaintance, containing certain proffers, which, with returning reflection, they found they could not with propriety retract. It made some of them do the wisest acts that ever they did in their lives.

This brings me to an anecdote which I must relate, though with little credit to myself; one that I never call to mind without its exciting feelings of respect, admiration, and gratitude. I formerly mentioned that I had quarrelled with Sir Walter Scott. It is true, I had all the quarrel on my own side: no matter for that; I was highly offended, exceedingly angry, and shunned all communication with him for a twelve-month. He heard that I was ill, and that my trouble had assumed a dangerous aspect. Every day, on his return from the Parliament-House, he called at Messrs. Grieve and Scott's to inquire

E

after my health, with much friendly solicitude; and this, too, after I had renounced his friendship, and told him that I held both it and his literary talents in contempt! One day in particular, he took Mr. Grieve aside, and asked him if I had proper attendants and an able physician. Mr. Grieve assured him that I was carefully attended, and had the skill of a professional gentleman, in whom I had the most implicit confidence. "I would fain have called," said he, "but I knew not how I would be received. I request, however, that he may have every proper attendance, and want for nothing that can contribute to the restoration of his health. And in particular, I have to request that you will let no pecuniary consideration whatever prevent his having the best medical advice in Edinburgh, for I shall see it paid. Poor Hogg! I would not for all that I am worth in the world that any thing serious should befall him."

As Mr. Grieve had been enjoined, he never mentioned this circumstance to me. I accidentally, however, came to the knowledge of it some months afterwards. I then questioned him as to the truth of it, when he told me it all, very much affected. I went straight home, and wrote an apology to Sir Walter, which was heartily received, and he invited me to breakfast next morning, adding, that he was longing much to see me. The same day, as we were walking round St. Andrew's Square, I endeavoured to make the cause of our difference the subject of conversation, but he eluded it. I tried it again some days afterwards, sitting in his study, but he again parried it with equal dexterity; so that I have been left to conjecture what could be his motive in refusing so peremptorily the trifle that I had asked of him. I know him too well to have the least suspicion that there could be any selfish or unfriendly feeling in the determination that he adopted, and I can account for it in no other way, than by supposing that he thought it mean in me to attempt either to acquire gain, or a name, by the efforts of other men; and that it was much more honourable, to use a proverb of his own, "that every herring should hang by its own head."

Mr. Wilson once drove me also into an ungovernable rage, by turning a long and elaborate poem of mine, on "The Field of Waterloo," into ridicule, on learning which I sent him a letter, which I thought was a tickler. There was scarcely an abusive epithet in our language that I did not call him by. My letter, however, had not the designed effect: the opprobrious names proved only a source of amusement to Wilson, and he sent me a letter of explanation and apology, which knit my heart closer to him than ever. My friends in general have been of opinion that he has amused himself and the public too often at my expense; but, except in one instance, which terminated very ill for me, and in which I had no more concern than the man in the moon, I never discerned any evil design on his part, and thought it all excellent sport. At the same time, I must acknowledge, that it was using too much freedom with any author, to print his name in full, to poems, letters, and essays, which he himself never saw. I do not say that he has done this; but either he or some one else has done it many a time.

My next literary undertaking was the "Jacobite Relics of Scotland." Of this work it is proper to mention, that it was first proposed in the Highland Society of London, His Royal Highness the Duke of Sussex being in the chair; yet, for all that, the native Highlanders were so jealous of a Sassenach[87] coming plodding among them, gathering up their rebellious scraps, that, had it not been for the influence of the ladies over the peasantry of their respective districts, I could never have succeeded. But, in the end, I am sure I produced two volumes of Jacobite Relics, such as no man in Scotland or England could have produced but myself. I assert it, and can prove it; for besides the songs and histories of events and persons, I collected all the original airs over a whole kingdom, many of them among a people whose language I did not understand; and that work I dedicated to the Highland Society of London in a poetical epistle.[88]

I published the first volume in 1819, reserving the second volume until the following year,[89] in the hope of collecting every remnant that was worthy of preservation. The task was exceedingly troublesome, but far from being unmixed with pleasure. The jealousy of the Highlanders was amusing beyond conception. I shall never forget with what sly and disdainful looks Donald would eye me, when I told him I was gathering up old songs. And then he would say, "Ohon, man, you surely haif had very less to do at home; and so you want to get some of the songs of the poor repellioners from me; and then you will give me up to King Shorge to be hanged? Hoo, no!—Cot tamn!—that will never do."[90]

[87] Gaelic for Saxon, that is an Englishman or Lowland Scot.

[88] *Of this work it is proper to mention . . . poetical epistle.* Added in AT.

[89] The *Jacobite Relics*, second series, was in fact published in 1821.

[90] *The jealousy of the Highlanders . . . never do.* Added in AT. Hogg frequently uses "Donald" as a general name for Highlanders.

In the interim between the publication of the first and second volumes I collected and arranged for publication "The Winter Evening Tales," which were published by Oliver and Boyd in 1820, in two volumes, closely printed. The greater part of these Tales was written in early life, when I was serving as a shepherd lad among the mountains, and on looking them over, I saw well enough that there was a blunt rusticity about them; but I liked them the better for it, and altered nothing. To me they appeared not only more characteristic of the life that I then led, but also of the manners that I was describing. As to the indelicacies hinted at by some reviewers, I do declare that such a thought never entered into my mind, so that the public are indebted for these indelicacies to the acuteness of the discoverers. Wo be to that reader who goes over a simple and interesting tale fishing for indelicacies, without calculating on what is natural for the characters with whom he is conversing; a practice, however, too common among people of the present age, especially if the author be not a blue-stocking. All that I can say for myself in general is, that I am certain I never intentionally meant ill, and that I hope to be forgiven, both by God and man, for every line that I have written injurious to the cause of religion, of virtue, or of good manners. On the other hand, I am so ignorant of the world, that it can scarcely be expected I should steer clear of all inadvertencies.

The following list of works may appear trifling in the eyes of some, but when it is considered that they have been produced by a man almost devoid of education, and principally, in his early days, debarred from every advantage in life, and possessed only of a quick eye in observing the operations of nature, it is certainly a sufficient excuse for inserting them here, more especially as some of them run a great risk of being lost. I am proud of it myself, and I do not deny it; nor is there one in the list, for the contents of which I have any reason to blush, when all things are taken into account. I was forty years of age before I wrote the "Queen's Wake." That poem was published in 1813; so that in that and the next six years I wrote and published

	Vols.
The Queen's Wake	I
Pilgrims of the Sun	I
The Hunting of Badlewe	I
Mador of the Moor	I
Poetic Mirror	I

Vols.

Dramatic Tales 2
Brownie of Bodsbeck 2
Winter Evening Tales 2
Sacred Melodies 1
Border Garland, No. I 1
Jacobite Relics of Scotland 2

Making fifteen volumes in seven years, besides many articles in periodical works. To these may now be added

Vols.

The Spy 1
Queen Hynde 1
The Three Perils of Man 3
The Three Perils of Women 3
Confessions of a Sinner 1
The Shepherd's Calendar 2
A Selection of Songs 1
The Queer Book 1
The Royal Jubilee 1
The Mountain Bard 1
The Forest Minstrel 1

Making in all about thirty volumes, which, if the quality were at all proportioned to the quantity, are enough for any man's life.⁹¹

I omitted to mention formerly, that in 1815, I was applied to by a celebrated composer of music, in the name of a certain company in London, to supply verses, suiting some ancient Hebrew Melodies, selected in the synagogues of Germany. I proffered to furnish them at a guinea a stanza, which was agreed to at once, and I furnished verses to them all. The work was published in a splendid style, price one guinea; but it was a hoax upon me, for I was never paid a farthing.

In this short Memoir, which is composed of extracts from a larger detail, I have confined myself to such anecdotes only as relate to my progress as a writer, and these I intend to continue from year to year as long as I live. There is much that I have written which cannot as yet appear; for the literary men of Scotland, my contemporaries, may change their characters, so as to forfeit the estimate at which I have set them, and my social companions may alter their habits. Of

⁹¹ *Making fifteen . . . man's life.* Added in AT.

my own productions, I have endeavoured to give an opinion, with perfect candour; and, although the partiality of an author may be too apparent in the preceding pages, yet I trust every generous heart will excuse, and make due allowance for the failing.[92]

REMINISCENCES OF FORMER DAYS

I MUST now proceed with my reminiscences at random, as from the time the last journal was finished and published I ceased keeping any notes. From 1809 until 1814 I resided in Edinburgh, having no home or place of retirement in my native district of Ettrick Forest, a want which I felt grievously in summer. But in the course of the last-mentioned year I received a letter from the late Duke Charles of Buccleugh, by the hands of his chamberlain, presenting me with the small farm of Altrive Lake, in the wilds of Yarrow.[1] The boon was quite unsolicited and unexpected, and never was a more welcome one conferred on an unfortunate wight, as it gave me once more a habitation among my native moors and streams, where each face was that of a friend, and each house was a home, as well as a residence for life to my aged father.

The letter was couched in the kindest terms, and informed me that I had long had a secret and sincere friend whom I knew not of, in his late Duchess, who had in her lifetime solicited such a residence

---

[92] 21 ends at this point.

[1] Hogg wrote to the Duchess of Buccleuch as follows in March 1814:

I know you will be thinking that this long prelude is to end with a request: No, madam! I have taken the resolution of never making another request. I will however tell you a story, which is, I believe, founded on a fact:—

There is a small farm at the head of a water called —— possessed by a mean fellow named ——. A third of it has been taken off and laid into another farm—the remainder is as yet unappropriated. Now, there is a certain poor bard, who has two old parents, each of them upwards of eighty-four years of age; and that bard has no house nor home to shelter those poor parents in, or cheer the evening of their lives. A single line from a certain very great and beautiful lady, to a certain Mr Riddle, would insure that small pendicle to the bard at once. But she will grant no such thing! I appeal to your grace if she is not a very bad lady that!—I am your grace's ever obliged and grateful

JAMES HOGG,
The Ettrick Shepherd.

(Quoted in E. C. Batho, *The Ettrick Shepherd* (Cambridge, 1927), p. 77–8.) The Duchess died five months later, but before her death she had expressed to the Duke her hope that Hogg would receive one of the Buccleuch farms. After her death the Duke fulfilled her wish by granting Hogg the farm of Altrive Lake in January 1815.

for me. In the letter he said, "The rent shall be nominal;" but it has not even been nominal, for such a thing as rent has never once been mentioned. Subsequently to that period I was a frequent guest at his Grace's table; and, as he placed me always next him, on his right hand, I enjoyed a good share of his conversation, and I must say of my benefactor, that I have never met with any man whom I deemed his equal. There is no doubt that he was beloved and esteemed, not only by his family and friends, but by all who could appreciate merit; yet, strange to say, Duke Charles was not popular among his tenantry. This was solely owing to the change of times, over which no nobleman can have any controul, and which it is equally impossible for him to redress; for a more considerate, benevolent, and judicious gentleman I never saw. It is natural to suppose that I loved him, and felt grateful towards him; but exclusive of all feelings of *that* nature, if I am any judge of mankind, Duke Charles had every qualification both of heart and mind, which ought to endear a nobleman to high and low, rich and poor. From the time of his beloved partner's death his spirits began to droop; and, though for the sake of his family he made many efforts to keep them up, the energy that formerly had supported them was broken, and the gnawings of a disconsolate heart brought him to an untimely grave.[2] Blessed be the memory of my two noble and only benefactors! they were lovely in their lives, and in their deaths they were but shortly divided.

I then began and built a handsome cottage on my new farm, and forthwith made it my head-quarters. But not content with this, having married in 1820 Miss Margaret Phillips, youngest daughter of Mr. Phillips, late of Longbridge-moor, in Annandale, and finding that I had then in the hands of Mr. Murray, Mr. Blackwood, Messrs. Oliver and Boyd, and Messrs. Longman and Co., debts due, or that would soon be due, to the amount of a thousand pounds, I determined once more to farm on a larger scale, and expressed my wish to the Right Honourable Lord Montague,[3] head trustee on his nephew's domains. His lordship readily offered me the farm of Mount-Benger, which adjoined my own. At first I determined not to accept of it, as it had ruined two well qualified farmers in the preceding six years; but was persuaded at last by some neighbours, in opposition to my own judgment, to accept of it, on the plea that the

[2] Duke Charles, the fourth Duke of Buccleuch, died on 20 April 1819.

[3] Lord Montagu (1776–1845) was the younger brother of the fourth Duke of Buccleuch, and acted as guardian to his nephew, the fifth Duke, during his minority.

farmers on the Buccleugh estate were never suffered to be great losers, and that at all events, if I could not *make* the rent, I could write for it. So accordingly I took a lease of the farm for nine years.

I called in my debts, which were all readily paid, and amounted to within a few pounds of one thousand; but at that period the sum was quite inadequate, the prices of ewes bordering on thirty shillings per head. The farm required stocking to the amount of one thousand sheep, twenty cows, five horses, farming utensils of all sorts, crop, manure, and, moreover, draining, fencing, and building, so that I soon found I had not half enough of money; and though I realized by writing, in the course of the next two years, seven hundred and fifty pounds, beside smaller sums paid in cash, yet I got into diffi-culties at the very first, out of which I could never redeem myself till the end of the lease, at which time live stock of all kinds having declined one half in value, the speculation left me once more without a sixpence in the world—and at the age of sixty it is fully late enough to begin it anew.

It will be consolatory however to my friends to be assured that none of these reverses ever preyed in the smallest degree on my spirits. As long as I did all for the best, and was conscious that no man could ever accuse me of dishonesty, I laughed at the futility of my own calculations, and let my earnings go as they came, amid contentment and happiness, determined to make more money as soon as possible, although it should go the same way.

One may think, on reading over this Memoir, that I must have worn out a life of misery and wretchedness; but the case has been quite the reverse. I never knew either man or woman who has been so uniformly happy as I have been; which has been partly owing to a good constitution, and partly from the conviction that a heavenly gift, conferring the powers of immortal song, was inherent in my soul. Indeed so uniformly smooth and happy has my married life been, that on a retrospect I cannot distinguish one part from another, save by some remarkably good days of fishing, shooting, and curling on the ice. Those who desire to peruse my youthful love adventures will find some of the best of them in those of "George Cochrane," in the following tales.[4]

Now, as I think the best way of writing these by-gone reminis-cences is to finish the subject one is on, before beginning another, I must revert to several circumstances of importance to no body but

[4] That is, the *Atrive Tales.*

myself. In 1822, perceiving that I was likely to run short of money, I began and finished in the course of a few months, "The Three Perils of Man, viz. War, Women, and Witchcraft!"[5] Lord preserve us! what a medley I made of it! for I never in my life rewrote a page of prose; and being impatient to get hold of some of Messrs. Longman and Co.'s money or their bills, which were the same, I dashed on, and mixed up with what might have been made one of the best historical tales our country ever produced, such a mass of diablerie as retarded the main story, and rendered the whole perfectly ludicrous. But the worst thing of all effected by this novel, or at least by the novel part of an authentic tale, was its influencing the ingenious Allan Cunningham to follow up the idea, and improve the subject; whereas, he made matters rather worse.[6] I received one hundred and fifty pounds for the edition of one thousand copies as soon as it was put to press. The house never manifested the least suspicion of me, more than if I had been one of their own firm.

The next year I produced "The Three Perils of Women,"[7] also in three volumes, and received the same price likewise, in bills, as soon as it was put to press. There is a good deal of pathos and absurdity in both the tales of this latter work; but I was all this while writing as if in desperation, and see matters now in a different light.

The next year, 1824, I published "The Confessions of a Sinner;" but it being a story replete with horror, after I had written it I durst not venture to put my name to it:[8] so it was published anonymously, and of course did not sell very well—so at least I believe, for I do not remember ever receiving any thing for it, and I am sure if there had been a reversion I should have had a moiety. However, I never

[5] Published by Longman in three volumes, 1822.

[6] In his *Sir Michael Scott* (1828).

[7] Published by Longman in three volumes, 1823.

[8] Hogg, in a letter to Blackwood of 28 June 1824, writes that the *Confessions* are likely to be reviewed in the *Noctes Ambrosianae*, and he asks Blackwood that "our friends" "will not notice them at all *as mine* but as written by *a Glasgow man* by all means". He continues that his anonyminity "will give excellent and delightful scope and freedom" (National Library of Scotland MS. 4012, f. 184–5). In his masterpiece Hogg, a devout presbyterian, attacks the extreme and deformed Calvinism of the kind depicted by Burns in "Holy Willie's Prayer". This is scarcely a theme the public would have expected of "the Ettrick Shepherd", and Hogg's desire for the "scope and freedom" of anonymity is easy to understand. The *Confessions* were not highly regarded in Hogg's lifetime, and this perhaps explains his unwillingness to dwell on the subject in the *Memoir*.

asked any thing; so on that point there was no misunderstanding.
Perhaps I may bring the parties to account for it still, which they
will like very ill.

But the same year I offered them two volumes 12mo of "The Lives
of Eminent Men;"⁹ to which they answered, "that my last publication had been found fault with in some very material points, and
they begged leave to decline publishing the present one until they
consulted some other persons with regard to its merits." Oho! thinks
I, since my favourite publishers thus think proper to take two
thousand volumes for nothing, ("Queen Hynde" and the "Confessions of a Sinner,") and then refuse the third, it is time to give them
up; so I never wrote another letter to that house.

I confess that there was a good deal of wrangling between Mr.
Blackwood and me with regard to a hundred pound bill of Messrs.
Longman and Co.'s, advanced on the credit of these works. When
Mr. Blackwood came to be a sharer in them, and to find that he was
likely to be a loser of that sum, or a great part of it, he caused me to
make over a bill to him of the same amount, which he afterwards
charged me with, and deducted from our subsequent transactions:—
so that, as far as ever I could be made to understand the matter, after
many letters and arguments, I never received into my own hand one
penny for these two works. I do not accuse Mr. Blackwood of dishonesty; on the contrary, with all his faults, I never saw any thing
but honour and integrity about him. But this was the fact. Messrs.
Longman and Co. advanced me one hundred pounds on the credit
of one or both of the works: I drew the money for the note, or rather
I believe Mr. Blackwood drew it out of the bank for me. But he
compelled me, whether I would or not, to grant him my promissory
note for the same sum, and I was to have a moiety of the proceeds
from both houses. The account was carried on against me till finally
obliterated; but the proceeds I never heard of; and yet, on coming
to London, I find that Messrs. Longman and Co. have not a copy
of either of the works, nor have had any for a number of years. It is
probable that they may have sold them off at a trade sale, and at a
very cheap rate too; but half of the edition was mine, and they ought
to have consulted me, or, at least, informed me of the transaction.
It was because I had an implicit confidence in Blackwood's honour
that I signed the bill, though I told him I could not comprehend it.
The whole of that trifling business has to this day continued a

⁹ Never published.

complete mystery to me. I have told the plain truth, and if any of the parties can explain it away I shall be obliged to them. If the money should ever by any chance drop in, "better late than never" will be my salutation.

In 1822 I bargained with Constable and Co. for an edition of my best poems in four volumes, for which they were to pay me two hundred pounds. It was with Mr. Robert Cadell[10] that I made the bargain. He was always a near and intimate friend of mine, but one whom at our club we reckoned a perfect Nabal; and in all our social parties we were wont to gibe him about his niggardly hardness, which he never took the least amiss. He offered not the smallest objection to the conditions; but he made a reserve (as I needed a bill at a short date) that if there were not above five hundred copies of the work sold when the bill became due, he was entitled to a renewal of the bill for six months. Accordingly, I attended the day before the bill became due and offered to accept of the renewal. Cadell took up the missive, read it over, and standing upright, he lifted his large eyes toward the cornice, his pale face looking more cadaverous than usual. He then conversed shortly with Mr. Fyffe, his cashier, studied the letter again for a good while, and then said, "And what are you going to do with the money, Hogg, that you draw out of the bank to-day on our bill?"

"I am gaun to bring it to you ye see," says I, "to lift the other bill wi'. An' I'll pay the four per centage out o' my ain pouch[11] wi' great cheerfulness, for the good I hae gotten o' the siller."[12]

"You have got full payment for the edition, have you?"

"Yes, I hae. Think ye I'm gaun to deny that?"

"And what did you do with it?"

"Od man, ye're no blate to speer.[13] But the truth is that I gae it away in rent."

"Then you have no chance ever to get it again?"

"Deil a grain."

"And do you consider that by this transaction you will change the sterling value that is already in your hand for our paper?"

"Ay, an' excepting the bit interest they are the very same to me."

[10] Robert Cadell (1788–1849) was the partner of Archibald Constable from 1811 to 1826; he obtained the copyright of Sir Walter Scott's novels in 1827.

[11] *pouch*   pocket.

[12] *siller*   money.

[13] *no blate to speer*   not reticent in asking.

"But, Hoggy, my man, I won't trust you to make the experiment. There's your missive. Keep hold of what you have, and I'll pay the bill when it is presented."

"There are some waur chaps than Bob Cadell, for as sairly as I hae misca'd[14] him whiles," thought I, as I went down stairs.

I have recorded every word that passed here, for I thought very highly of his conduct at the time; and when I saw what soon after followed,[15] I thought ten times more of it, and never reported Cadell as a scrub again. Sir Walter Scott at the same time sent me a credit order on his banker for a hundred pounds for fear of any embarrassment; so that altogether I find I lost upwards of two thousand pounds on Mount-Benger lease,—a respectable sum for an old shepherd to throw away.

Having been so much discouraged by the failure of "Queen Hynde,"[16] I gave up all thoughts of ever writing another long poem but continued for six years to write fairy tales, ghost stories, songs, and poems for periodicals of every description, sometimes receiving beral payment, and sometimes none, just as the editor or proprietor, felt disposed. It will be but justice to give a list of such as pay and such as do not, and their several grades, which I may add to this by and by.

In 1829 Baillie Blackwood published a selection of my best songs that could be recovered, with notes, consisting of about one hundred and forty.[17] The work was exceedingly well received, and has paid me a good sum already. In the following year, that is, the year before last, the baillie also ventured to *print* one thousand copies of a miscellaneous work of mine, which, for fear of that great bugbear REFORM, he has never dared to publish, and I am convinced never will.

I have had many dealings with that gentleman, and have been often obliged to him, and yet I think he has been as much obliged to me, perhaps a good deal more, and I really believe in my heart that

---

[14] *misca'd* slandered, disparaged.

[15] Hogg refers to the financial crash which brought about the bankruptcy of the house of Constable and the ruin of Scott in January 1826.

[16] Published 1825.

[17] This book was in fact published in 1831, not 1829. Hogg perhaps changed this date in order to throw a more favourable light on his quarrel with Blackwood over the publication of *Altrive Tales* (1832). Hogg gives the correct date of the 1831 *Songs* on p. 15 of the *Memoir*.

he is as much disposed to be friendly to me as to any man; but there is another principle that circumscribes that feeling in all men, and into very narrow limits in some. It is always painful to part with one who has been a benefactor even on a small scale, but there are some things that no independent heart can bear. The great fault of Blackwood is, that he regards no man's temper or disposition; but the more he can provoke an author by insolence and contempt, he likes the better. Besides, he will never once confess that he is in the wrong, else any thing might be forgiven; no, no, the thing is impossible that he can ever be wrong! The poor author is not only always in the wrong, but, "Oh, he is the most insufferable beast!"

What has been the consequence? He has driven all his original correspondents from him that first gave Maga her zest, save one, who, though still his friend, can but seldom write for him, being now otherwise occupied, and another, who is indeed worth his weight in gold to him; but who, though invaluable, and I am sure much attached, yet has been a thousand times at the point of bolting off like a flash of lightning.[18] I know it well, and Ebony, for his own sake, had better take care of this last remaining stem of a goodly bush, for he may depend on it that he has only an eel by the tail.

For my part, after twenty years of feelings hardly suppressed, he has driven me beyond the bounds of human patience. That Magazine of his, which owes its rise principally to myself, has often put words and sentiments into my mouth of which I have been greatly ashamed, and which have given much pain to my family and relations, and many of those after a solemn written promise that such freedoms should never be repeated. I have been often urged to restrain and humble him by legal measures as an incorrigible offender deserves. I know I have it in my power, and if he dares me to the task, I want but a hair to make a tether of.

I omitted to mention that I wrote and published a Masque or Drama, comprehending many songs, that summer the king was in Scotland.[19] It was a theme that suited me to a tittle, as I there suffered fancy to revel free. Mr. Blackwood never gave me any thing for it; but I got what I held in higher estimation, his Majesty's

[18] Lockhart was by this time "otherwise occupied" as the editor of the *Quarterly Review*, although he still made occasional contributions to *Blackwood's*. Wilson was still associated with Blackwood, who figured in the "Chaldee Manuscript" as "Ebony".

[19] *The Royal Jubilee*, published by Blackwood in 1822.

thanks, for that and my other loyal and national songs. The note is written by Sir Robert Peel, in his Majesty's name, and I have preserved it as a relic.

In the spring of 1829 I first mentioned the plan of the "Altrive Tales" to Mr. Blackwood in a letter. He said, in answer, that the publication of them would be playing a sure card, if Mr. Lockhart would edit them. He and I waited on Mr. Lockhart subsequently, at Chiefswood,[20] and proposed the plan to him. He said that he would cheerfully assist me both in the selection and correction, but that it was altogether without a precedent for one author to publish an edition of the works of another while the latter was still alive, and better qualified than any other person to arrange the work. Blackwood then requested me to begin writing and arranging forthwith, that we might begin publishing about the end of the year. But when the end of the year came, he put off and put off until the next spring, and then desired me to continue my labours till November next, as I should still be making the work the better, and would ultimately profit by so doing. Then when last November came, he answered a letter of mine in very bad humour, stating that he would neither advance me money on the work that had lain a year unpublished, nor commence a new work in a time of such agitation—and that I *must not* think of it for another year at least.

I then began to suspect that the whole pretence had all along been only a blind to keep me from London, whither I had proposed going, and keep me entirely in his own power. So, rather than offer the series to any other Scottish bookseller, I carried it at once to London, where it was cordially accepted on my own terms, without the intervention or assistance of any body. It was not without the greatest reluctance that I left my family in the wilderness; but I had no alternative. It behoved me either to remain there and starve, or try my success in the metropolis of the empire, where I could have the assistance of more than one friend on whose good taste and critical discernment I could implicitly rely.[21]

In the following volumes I purpose to give the grave and gay tales, the romantic and the superstitious, alternately, as far as is

[20] Lockhart's cottage near Abbotsford.

[21] Hogg hoped that the *Altrive Tales* would follow the success of Cadell's collected edition of the Waverly Novels (1829–33), and that this would give his family financial security after his death. The first volume, which contains the *Memoir*, was well received, but no further volumes appeared because of the bankruptcy of the publisher, Cochrane.

consistent with the size of each volume. At all events I think I can promise my readers that I shall present them with a series of stories which they shall scarcely feel disposed to lay aside until a rainy Sunday; and with a few reminiscences relating to eminent men, which I deem may be interesting to many, I once more bring this Memoir, it may be hoped, to a partial conclusion.

SIR WALTER SCOTT[22]

One fine day in the summer of 1801,[23] as I was busily engaged working in the field at Ettrick House, Wat Shiel came over to me and said, that "I boud gang away down to the Ramseycleuch as fast as my feet could carry me, for there war some gentlemen there wha wantit to speak to me."

"Wha can be at the Ramseycleuch that want me, Wat?"

"I couldna say, for it wasna me that they spak to i' the byganging. But I'm thinking it's the Shirra an' some o' his gang."

I was rejoiced to hear this, for I had seen the first volumes of the "Minstrelsy of the Scottish Border," and had copied a number of old ballads from my mother's recital, and sent them to the editor preparatory for a third volume. I accordingly went towards home to put on my Sunday clothes, but before reaching it I met with THE SHIRRA and Mr. William Laidlaw coming to visit me. They alighted and remained in our cottage for a space better than an hour, and my mother chanted the ballad of Old Maitlan' to them, with which Mr. Scott was highly delighted. I had sent him a copy, (not a very perfect one, as I found afterwards, from the singing of another Laidlaw), but I thought Mr. Scott had some dread of a part being forged, that had been the cause of his journey into the wilds of Ettrick. When he heard my mother sing it he was quite satisfied, and I remember he asked her if she thought it had ever been printed; and her answer was, "Oo, na, na, sir, it was never printed i' the world, for my brothers an' me learned it frae auld Andrew Moor,

[22] This is a reprint, with some minor alterations in the wording and one long insertion (see below), of Hogg's "Reminiscences of Former Days. My First Interview with Sir Walter Scott", *Edinburgh Literary Journal*, vol. 2 (1829), p. 51–2. There is evidence that Hogg met Scott (probably briefly) for the first time two or three months before the meeting described here (see Strout, *Life and Letters of James Hogg*, p. 29–30).

[23] The meeting Hogg describes here took place in July 1802, not in 1801 (see Johnson, *Sir Walter Scott: the Great Unknown*, vol. 1, p. 191). There are some minor differences between Hogg's account of this meeting and that given by William Laidlaw (published in the *Transactions of the Hawick Archaeological Society* (1905), p. 66–74).

an' he learned it, an' mony mae, frae auld Baby Mettlin, that was housekeeper to the first laird o' Tushilaw."

"Then that must be a very auld story, indeed, Margaret," said he.

"Ay, it is that! It is an auld story! But mair nor that, except George Warton and James Steward, there was never ane o' my sangs prentit till ye prentit them yoursell, an' ye hae spoilt them a'thegither. They war made for singing, an' no for reading; and they 're nouther right spelled nor right setten down."

"Heh—heh—heh! Take ye that, Mr. Scott," said Laidlaw.

Mr. Scott answered by a hearty laugh, and the recital of a verse, but I have forgot what it was, and my mother gave him a rap on the knee with her open hand, and said "It is true enough, for a' that."

We were all to dine at Ramseycleuch with the Messrs. Brydon; but Mr. Scott and Mr. Laidlaw went away to look at something before dinner, and I was to follow. On going into the stable-yard at Ramseycleuch, I met with Mr. Scott's liveryman, a far greater original than his master, at whom I asked if the Shirra was come?

"O, ay, lad, the Shirra's come," said he. "Are ye the chiel that maks the auld ballads and sings them?"

"I said I fancied I was he that he meant, though I had never made ony very *auld* ballads."

"Ay, then, lad, gae your ways in an' speir for the Shirra. They'll let ye see where he is. He 'll be very glad to see you."

During the sociality of the evening, the discourse ran very much on the different breeds of sheep, that curse of the community of Ettrick Forest. The original black-faced forest breed being always called *the short sheep*, and the Cheviot breed *the long sheep*, the disputes at that period ran very high about the practicable profits of each. Mr. Scott, who had come into that remote district to preserve what fragments remained of its legendary lore, was rather bored with the everlasting question of the long and the short sheep. So at length, putting on his most serious calculating face, he turned to Mr. Walter Brydon and said, "I am rather at a loss regarding the merits of this *very* important question. How long must a sheep actually measure to come under the denomination of *a long sheep*?"

Mr. Brydon, who, in the simplicity of his heart, neither perceived the quiz nor the reproof, fell to answer with great sincerity,—"It's the woo, sir—it's the woo that makes the difference. The lang sheep hae the short woo, and the short sheep hae the lang thing; and these are just kind o' names we gie them like." Mr. Scott could not preserve his grave face of strict calculation; it went gradually awry, and a hearty guffaw followed. When I saw the very same words repeated near the beginning of the Black Dwarf, how could I be mistaken of the author? It is true, Johnnie Ballantyne persuaded me into a nominal belief of the contrary, for several years following, but I could never get the better of that and several similar coincidences.

The next day we went off, five in number, to visit the wilds of Rankleburn, to see if on the farms of Buccleuch there were any relics of the Castles of Buccleuch or Mount-Comyn, the ancient and original possession of the Scotts. We found no remains of either tower or fortalice, save an old chapel and church-yard, and a mill and mill-dam, where corn never grew, but where, as old Satchells very appropriately says,

> Had heather-bells been corn of the best,
> The Buccleuch mill would have had a noble grist.[24]

It must have been used for grinding the chief's black mails, which, it is known, were all paid to him in kind. Many of these still continue to be paid in the same way; and if report say true, he would be the better of a mill and kiln on some part of his land at this day, as well as a sterling conscientious miller to receive and render.

Besides having been mentioned by Satchells, there was a remaining tradition in the country that there was a font stone of blue marble, out of which the ancient heirs of Buccleuch were baptized, covered up among the ruins of the old church. Mr. Scott was curious to see if we could discover it; but on going among the ruins we found the rubbish at the spot, where the altar was known to have been, dug out to the foundation,—we knew not by whom, but no font had been found. As there appeared to have been a kind of recess in the eastern gable, we fell a turning over some loose stones, to see if the font was not concealed there, when we came to one half of a small pot, encrusted thick with rust. Mr. Scott's eyes brightened, and he swore it was an ancient consecrated helmet. Laidlaw, however, scratching it minutely out, found it covered with a layer of pitch inside, and then said, "Ay, the truth is, sir, it is neither mair nor less than a piece of a tar pat that some o' the farmers hae been buisting their sheep out o', i' the auld kirk langsyne." Sir Walter's shaggy eyebrows

---

[24] This quotation is from *A Metrical History of the Honourable Families of the Name of Scot and Elliot in the Shires of Roxburgh and Selkirk*, by Captain Walter Scot of Satchells. This work was printed in 1688 and again in 1776.

F

dipped deep over his eyes, and suppressing a smile, he turned and strode away as fast as he could, saying, that "we had just rode all the way to see that there was nothing to *be* seen."

I remember his riding upon a terribly high-spirited horse, which had the perilous fancy of leaping every drain, rivulet, and ditch that came in our way; the consequence was, that he was everlastingly bogging himself, while sometimes the rider kept his seat despite of the animal's plunging, and at other times he was obliged to extricate himself the best way he could. In coming through a place called the Milsey Bog, I said to him, "Mr. Scott, that's the maddest deil of a beast I ever saw. Can ye no gar him tak a wee mair time? He's just out o' ae lair intil another wi' ye."

"Ay," said he, "he and I have been very often, these two days past, like the Pechs; we could stand straight up and tie our shoe-lachets." I did not understand the joke, nor do I yet, but I think these were his words.

We visited the old castles of Thirlestane and Tushilaw, and dined and spent the afternoon, and the night, with Mr. Brydon of Crosslee. Sir Walter was all the while in the highest good-humour, and seemed to enjoy the range of mountain solitude, which we traversed, exceedingly. Indeed, I never saw him otherwise, in the fields. On the rugged mountains—or even toiling in Tweed to the waist, I have seen his glee not only surpass his own, but that of all other men. His memory, or, perhaps, I should say, his recollection, surpasses that of all men whom I ever knew. I saw a pleasant instance of it recorded lately, regarding Campbell's "Pleasures of Hope;" but I think I can relate a more extraordinary one.

He and Skene of Rubislaw and I were out one night, about midnight, leistering[25] kippers in Tweed, and, on going to kindle a light at the Elibank March, we found, to our inexpressible grief, that our coal had gone out. To think of giving up our sport was out of the question; so we had no other shift, save to send Rob Fletcher home, all the way through the darkness, the distance of two miles, for another fiery peat.

While Fletcher was absent, we three sat down on a piece of beautiful greensward, on the brink of the river, and Scott desired me to sing him my ballad of "Gilmanscleuch." Now, be it remembered, that this ballad had never been either printed or penned. I had

---

[25] *leistering* striking at and catching salmon with a spear with three or more barbed prongs.

merely composed it by rote, and, on finishing it, three years before, I had sung it once over to Sir Walter. I began it at his request; but, at the eighth or ninth verse, I stuck in it, and could not get on with another line; on which he began it a second time, and recited it every word from beginning to end. It being a very long ballad, consisting of eighty-eight stanzas, I testified my astonishment. He said that he had lately been out on a pleasure party on the Forth, and that, to amuse the company, he had recited both that ballad and one of Southey's, ("The Abbot of Aberbrothock,") both of which ballads he had only heard once from their respective authors, and he believed he had recited them both without misplacing a word.

Rob Fletcher came at last, and old Laidlaw of the Peel with him, and into the foaming river we plunged, in our frail bark, with a fine blazing light. In a few minutes we came into Gliddy's Weal, the deepest pool in Tweed, when we perceived that our boat gave evident symptoms of sinking. When Scott saw the terror that Peel was in, he laughed till the tears blinded his eyes. Always, the more mischief, the better sport for him! "For God's sake, push her to the side!" roared Peel. "Oh, she goes fine!" said Scott; "An' gin the boat were bottomless, an' seven miles to row;" and, by the time he had well got out the words, down she went to the bottom, plunging us all into Tweed over head and ears. It was no sport to me at all; but that was a glorious night for Sir Walter, and the next day was no worse.[26]

I remember leaving Altrive Lake once with him, accompanied by my dear friend William Laidlaw, and Sir Adam Fergusson, to visit the tremendous solitudes of The Grey Mare's Tail, and Loch Skene. I conducted them through that wild region by a path, which, if not rode by Clavers, was, I dare say, never rode by another gentleman.[27] Sir Adam rode inadvertently into a gulf, and got a sad fright; but Sir Walter, in the very worst paths, never dismounted, save at Loch Skene, to take some dinner. We went to Moffat that night, where

[26] *His memory, or, perhaps, I should say . . . no worse.* Not in the *Edinburgh Literary Journal* article; an addition made by Hogg for the *Altrive Tales* text.

[27] "Clavers" is John Graham of Claverhouse, Viscount Dundee. Hogg's novel of the Covenanters, *The Brownie of Bodsbeck*, is set in the region of Loch Skene, and includes an account of how Clavers rode over some tremendously precipitous ground in pursuit of a small group of Covenanters. "The marks of that infernal courser's feet are shewn to this day on a steep, nearly perpendicular, below the Bubbly Craig, along which he is said to have ridden at full speed" (*The Brownie of Bodsbeck* (Edinburgh) 1818, vol. 1, p. 167).

we met with some of his family, and such a day and night of glee I never witnessed. Our very perils were matter to him of infinite merriment; and then there was a short-tempered boot-boy at the inn, who wanted to pick a quarrel with him, at which he laughed till the water ran over his cheeks.

I was disappointed in never seeing some incident in his subsequent works laid in a scene resembling the rugged solitude around Loch Skene, for I never saw him survey any with so much attention. A single serious look at a scene generally filled his mind with it, and he seldom took another; but here he took the names of all the hills, their altitudes, and relative situations with regard to one another, and made me repeat them several times. It may occur in some of his works which I have not seen, and I think it will, for he has rarely ever been known to interest himself, either in a scene or a character, which did not appear afterwards in all its most striking peculiarities.

There are not above five people in the world who, I think, know Sir Walter better, or understand his character better than I do; and if I outlive him, which is likely, as I am five months and ten days younger, I shall draw a mental portrait of him, the likeness of which to the original shall not be disputed. In the mean time, this is only a reminiscence, in my own line, of an illustrious friend among the mountains.

The enthusiasm with which he recited, and spoke of our ancient ballads, during that first tour of his through the Forest, inspired me with a determination immediately to begin and imitate them, which I did, and soon grew tolerably good at it. I dedicated "The Mountain Bard" to him:—

> Bless'd be his generous heart for aye;
> He told me where the relic lay,
> Pointed my way with ready will,
> Afar on Ettrick's wildest hill;
> Watch'd my first notes with curious eye,
> And wonder'd at my minstrelsy:
> He little ween'd a parent's tongue
> Such strains had o'er my cradle sung.[28]

[28] These lines are from Hogg's *Queen's Wake*. After the poetic contest held in honour of Mary Queen of Scots, the Queen gives an ancient harp to the "Bard of Ettrick", who wins second place in the contest, and who is regarded by Hogg as the author of the traditional ballads of Ettrick and Yarrow. After this bard's death no one can tune the harp successfully, though Bangour, Ramsay and others try with indifferent success. The harp is then found and successfully tuned by Scott—"Walter the Abbot". The lines quoted appear at this point.

SOUTHEY

My first interview with Mr. Southey was at the Queen's Head inn, in Keswick, where I had arrived, wearied, one evening, on my way to Westmoreland; and not liking to intrude on his family circle that evening, I sent a note up to Greta Hall,[29] requesting him to come down and see me, and drink one half mutchkin along with me. He came on the instant, and stayed with me about an hour and a half. But I was a grieved as well as an astonished man, when I found that he refused all participation in my beverage of rum punch. For a poet to refuse his glass was to me a phenomenon; and I confess I doubted in my own mind, and doubt to this day, if perfect sobriety and transcendent poetical genius can exist together. In Scotland I am sure they cannot. With regard to the English, I shall leave them to settle that among themselves, as they have little that is worth drinking.

Before we had been ten minutes together my heart was knit to Southey, and every hour thereafter my esteem for him increased. I breakfasted with him next morning, and remained with him all that day and the next; and the weather being fine, we spent the time in rambling on the hills and sailing on the lake; and all the time he manifested a delightful flow of spirits, as well as a kind sincerity of manner, repeating convivial poems and ballads, and always between hands breaking jokes on his nephew, young Coleridge, in whom he seemed to take great delight. He gave me, with the utmost readiness, a poem and ballad of his own, for a work which I then projected. I objected to his going with Coleridge and me, for fear of encroaching on his literary labours; and, as I had previously resided a month at Keswick, I knew every scene almost in Cumberland; but he said he was an early riser, and never suffered any task to interfere with his social enjoyments and recreations; and along with us he went both days.

Southey certainly is as elegant a writer as any in the kingdom. But those who would love Southey as well as admire him, must see him, as I did, in the bosom, not only of one lovely family, but of three, all attached to him as a father, and all elegantly maintained and educated, it is generally said, by his indefatigable pen. The whole of

[29] Southey moved to Greta Hall, Keswick, in 1803 and made it his home for the rest of his life. In 1795 he had married Edith Fricker, whose sister became the wife of Coleridge. Greta Hall consisted of two houses under one roof, and Coleridge and his family moved into one of these houses in 1800. By 1809 Coleridge had practically left his family, and they became Southey's dependants.

Southey's conversation and economy, both at home and afield, left an impression of veneration on my mind, which no future contingency shall ever either extinguish or injure. Both his figure and countenance are imposing, and deep thought is strongly marked in his dark eye; but there is a defect in his eyelids, for these he has no power of raising; so that, when he looks up, he turns up his face, being unable to raise his eyes; and when he looks towards the top of one of his romantic mountains, one would think he was looking at the zenith. This peculiarity is what will most strike every stranger in the appearance of the accomplished laureate. He does not at all see well at a distance, which made me several times disposed to get into a passion with him, because he did not admire the scenes which I was pointing out. We have only exchanged a few casual letters since that period, and I have never seen this great and good man again.

WORDSWORTH

I have forgotten what year it was, but it was in the summer that the "Excursion" was first published,[30] when Mr. James Wilson[31] came to me, one day, in Edinburgh, and asked me to come to his mother's house in Queen Street to dinner, and meet Mr. Wordsworth and his lady. I said I should be glad to meet any friend of his kind and venerated mother's at any time, and should certainly come. But not having the least conception that the great poet of the Lakes was in Edinburgh, and James having called him *Mr.* Wordsworth, I took it for the celebrated horse-dealer of the same name, and entertained some shrewd misgivings, how he should chance to be a guest in a house where only the first people in Edinburgh were wont to be invited.

"You will like him very much," said James; "for although he proses a little, he is exceedingly intelligent."

"I dare say he is," returned I; "at all events, he is allowed to be a good judge of horse-flesh!" The Entomologist liked the joke well, and carried it on for some time; and I found, in my tour southward with the celebrated poet, that several gentlemen fell into the same error, expressing themselves as at a loss why I should be travelling the country with a *horse-couper*. He was clothed in a grey russet

[30] 1814.

[31] James Wilson, an eminent naturalist, was the brother of John Wilson, "Christopher North".

jacket and pantaloons, be it remembered, and wore a broad-brimmed beaver hat; so that to strangers he doubtless had a very original appearance.

When I finally learned from James that it was the poet of the Lakes whom I was to meet, I was overjoyed, for I admired many of his pieces exceedingly, though I had not then seen his ponderous "Excursion." I listened to him that night as to a superior being, far exalted above the common walks of life. His sentiments seemed just, and his language, though perhaps a little pompous, was pure, sentient, and expressive. We called on several noblemen and gentlemen in company; and all the while he was in Scotland I loved him better and better. Old Dr. Robert Anderson[32] travelled along with us as far as the sources of the Yarrow, and it was delightful to see the deference which Wordsworth paid to that venerable man. We went into my father's cot, and partook of some homely refreshment, visited St. Mary's Lake, which that day was calm, and pure as any mirror; and Mrs. Wordsworth in particular testified great delight with the whole scene. In tracing the windings of the pastoral Yarrow, from its source to its confluence with the sister stream, the poet was in great good-humour, delightful, and most eloquent. Indeed it was impossible to see Yarrow to greater advantage; and yet it failed of the anticipated inspiration; for "Yarrow Visited" is not so sweet or ingenious a poem as "Yarrow Unvisited;" so much is hope superior to enjoyment.

From Selkirk we were obliged to take different routes, as Wordsworth had business in Teviotdale, and I in Eskdale; and, at last, I landed at Ryedale Mount, his delightful dwelling, a day and a night before him and his lady. I found his sister there, however, a pure, ingenuous child of nature; kind, benevolent, and greatly attached to her brother. Her conversation was a true mental treat; and we spent the time with the children delightfully till the poet's arrival.

I dined with him, and called on him several times afterwards, and certainly never met with any thing but the most genuine kindness; therefore people have wondered why I should have indulged in caricaturing his style in the "Poetic Mirror."[33] I have often regretted

---

[32] Dr Robert Anderson (1750–1830), M. D. Edinburgh, edited *A Complete Edition of the Poets of Great Britain* in fourteen volumes (1792–5), and he was for a time the editor of the *Edinburgh Magazine*.

[33] *The Poetic Mirror* (1816) contains three parodies of Wordsworth which have been highly praised.

that myself; but it was merely a piece of ill-nature at an affront which I conceived had been put on me. It was the triumphal arch scene. This anecdote has been told and told again, but never truly; and was likewise brought forward in the "Noctes Ambrosianae," as a joke; but it was no joke; and the plain, simple truth of the matter was thus:—

It chanced one night, when I was there, that there was a resplendent arch across the zenith, from the one horizon to the other, of something like the aurora borealis, but much brighter. It was a scene that is well remembered, for it struck the country with admiration, as such a phenomenon had never before been witnessed in such perfection; and, as far as I could learn, it had been more brilliant over the mountains and pure waters of Westmoreland than any where else. Well, when word came into the room of the splendid meteor, we all went out to view it; and, on the beautiful platform at Mount Ryedale we were all walking, in twos and threes, arm-in-arm, talking of the phenomenon, and admiring it. Now, be it remembered, that Wordsworth, Professor Wilson,[34] Lloyd,[35] De Quincey, and myself, were present, besides several other literary gentlemen, whose names I am not certain that I remember aright. Miss Wordsworth's arm was in mine, and she was expressing some fears that the splendid stranger might prove ominous, when I, by ill luck, blundered out the following remark, thinking that I was saying a good thing:— "Hout, me'm! it is neither mair nor less than joost a treeumphal airch, raised in honour of the meeting of the poets."

"That's not amiss.—Eh? Eh?—that's very good," said the Professor, laughing. But Wordsworth, who had De Quincey's arm, gave a grunt, and turned on his heel, and leading the little opium-chewer aside, he addressed him in these disdainful and venomous words:—"Poets? Poets?—What does the fellow mean?—Where are they?"

Who could forgive this? For my part, I never can, and never will! I admire Wordsworth; as who does not, whatever they may pretend? but for that short sentence I have a lingering ill-will at him which I cannot get rid of. It is surely presumption in any man to circumscribe all human excellence within the narrow sphere of his own capacity. The "*Where are they?*" was too bad! I have always some

[34] John Wilson, "Christopher North", held the Chair of Moral Philosophy at Edinburgh University.

[35] Charles Lloyd (1768–1829), poet and friend of Coleridge.

hopes that De Quincey was *leeing*, for I did not myself hear Wordsworth utter the words.

I have only a single remark to make on the poetry of Wordsworth, and I do it because I never saw the remark made before. It relates to the richness of his works for quotations. For these they are a mine that is altogether inexhaustible. There is nothing in nature that you may not get a quotation out of Wordsworth to suit, and a quotation too that breathes the very soul of poetry. There are only three books in the world that are worth the opening in search of mottos and quotations, and all of them are alike rich. These are, the Old Testament, Shakspeare, and the poetical works of Wordsworth, and, strange to say, the "Excursion" abounds most in them.

ALLAN CUNNINGHAM [36]

One day, about the beginning of autumn, some three-and-twenty years ago, as I was herding my master's ewes on the great hill of Queensberry, in Nithsdale, I perceived two men coming towards me, who appeared to be strangers. I saw, by their way of walking, they were not shepherds, and could not conceive what the men were seeking there, where there was neither path nor aim towards any human habitation. However, I stood staring about me, till they came up, always ordering my old dog Hector to silence in an authoritative style, he being the only servant I had to attend to my orders. The men approached me rather in a breathless state, from climbing the hill. The one was a tall thin man, of a fairish complexion, and pleasant intelligent features, seemingly approaching to forty, and the other a dark ungainly youth of about eighteen, with a boardly[37] frame for his age, and strongly marked manly features—the very model of Burns, and exactly such a man. Had they been of the same age, it would not have been easy to distinguish the one from the other.

The eldest came up and addressed me frankly, asking me if I was Mr. Harkness's shepherd, and if my name was James Hogg? to both of which queries I answered cautiously in the affirmative, for I was afraid they were come to look after me with an accusation regarding some of the lasses. The younger stood at a respectful distance, as if I had been the Duke of Queensberry, instead of a ragged servant

[36] This is a reprint, with some minor alterations in the wording, of Hogg's "Reminiscences of Former Days. My First Interview with Allan Cunningham", *Edinburgh Literary Journal*, vol. 1 (1829), p. 374–5.
[37] *boardly* stalwart, "buirdly".

lad herding sheep. The other seized my hand, and said, "Well, then, sir, I am glad to see you. There is not a man in Scotland whose hand I am prouder to hold."

I could not say a single word in answer to this address; but when he called me SIR, I looked down at my bare feet and ragged coat, to remind the man whom he was addressing. But he continued: "My name is James Cunningham, a name unknown to you, though yours is not entirely so to me; and this is my younger brother Allan, the greatest admirer that you have on earth, and himself a young aspiring poet of some promise. You will be so kind as excuse this intrusion of ours on your solitude, for, in truth, I could get no peace either night or day with Allan, till I consented to come and see you."

I then stepped down the hill to where Allan Cunningham still stood, with his weather-beaten cheek toward me, and, seizing his hard brawny hand, I gave it a hearty shake, saying something as kind as I was able, and, at the same time, I am sure as stupid as it possibly could be. From that moment we were friends; for Allan has none of the proverbial Scottish caution about him; he is all heart together, without reserve either of expression or manner: you at once see the unaffected benevolence, warmth of feeling, and firm independence, of a man conscious of his own rectitude and mental energies. Young as he was, I had heard of his name, although slightly, and, I think, seen one or two of his juvenile pieces. Of an elder brother of his, Thomas Mouncey, I had, previous to that, conceived a very high idea, and I always marvel how he could possibly put his poetical vein under lock and key, as he did all at once; for he certainly then bade fair to be the first of Scottish bards.

I had a small bothy[38] upon the hill, in which I took my breakfast and dinner on wet days, and rested myself. It was so small, that we had to walk in on all-fours; and when we were in, we could not get up our heads any way, but in a sitting posture. It was exactly my own length, and, on the one side, I had a bed of rushes, which served likewise as a seat; on this we all three sat down, and there we spent the whole afternoon,—and, I am sure, a happier group of three never met on the hill of Queensberry. Allan brightened up prodigiously after he got into the dark bothy, repeating all his early pieces of poetry, and part of his brother's, to me. The two brothers partook heartily, and without reserve, of my scrip and bottle of

[38] *bothy*   a primitive dwelling or shelter, used especially of living-quarters for workmen; a shelter on a hillside for shepherds or climbers.

sweet milk, and the elder Mr. Cunningham had a strong bottle with him—I have forgot whether it was brandy or rum, but I remember it was excessively good, and helped to keep up our spirits to a late hour. Thus began at that bothy in the wilderness a friendship, and a mutual attachment between two aspiring Scottish peasants, over which the shadow of a cloud has never yet passed.

From that day forward I failed not to improve my acquaintance with the Cunninghams. I visited them several times at Dalswinton, and never missed an opportunity of meeting with Allan when it was in my power to do so. I was astonished at the luxuriousness of his fancy. It was boundless; but it was the luxury of a rich garden overrun with rampant weeds. He was likewise then a great mannerist in expression, and no man could mistake his verses for those of any other man. I remember seeing some imitations of Ossian by him, which I thought exceedingly good; and it struck me that that style of composition was peculiarly fitted for his vast and fervent imagination.

When Cromek's "Nithsdale and Galloway Relics" came to my hand, I at once discerned the strains of my friend, and I cannot describe with what sensations of delight I first heard Mr. Morrison read the "Mermaid of Galloway," while at every verse I kept naming the author. It had long been my fixed opinion, that if a person could once succeed in the genuine ballad style, his muse was adequate for any other; and after seeing Allan's strains in that work, I concluded that no man could calculate what he was capable of.

I continued my asseverations to all my intimate friends, *that Allan Cunningham was the author of all that was beautiful in the work.* Gray, who had an attachment to Cromek, denied it positively on his friend's authority. Grieve joined him. Morrison, I saw, had strong lurking suspicions; but then he stickled for the ancient genius of Galloway. When I went to Sir Walter Scott, (then Mr. Scott,) I found him decidedly of the same opinion as myself; and he said he wished to God we had that valuable and original young man fairly out of Cromek's hands again.

I next wrote a review of the work, in which I laid the saddle on the right horse, and sent it to Mr. Jeffrey;[39] but, after retaining it for some time, he returned it with a note, saying, that he had read over the article, and was convinced of the fraud which had been

[39] Editor of the *Edinburgh Review.* Hogg was correct in his speculations about Cunningham's part in Cromek's *Remains of Nithsdale and Galloway Song.*

attempted to be played off on the public, but he did not think it worthy of exposure. I have the article, and card, by me to this day.

Mr. Cunningham's style of poetry is greatly changed of late for the better. I have never seen any style improved so much. It is free of all that crudeness and mannerism that once marked it so decidedly. He is now uniformly lively, serious, descriptive, or pathetic, as he changes his subject; but formerly he jumbled all these together, as in a boiling caldron, and when once he began, it was impossible to calculate where or when he was going to end. If these reminiscences should meet his friendly eye, he will pardon them, on the score that they are the effusions of a heart that loves to dwell on some scenes of former days.

GALT

I first met with this most original and most careless writer at Greenock, in the summer of 1804, as I and two friends were setting out on a tour through the Hebrides; so that Galt and I have been acquainted these twenty-eight years.

That was a memorable evening for me, for it was the first time I ever knew that my name had been known beyond the precincts of my native wilds, and was not a little surprised at finding it so well known in a place called Greenock, at the distance of one hundred miles. I had by some chance heard the name of the town, and had formed an idea of its being a mouldy-looking village, on an ugly coast. How agreeably was I deceived, not only in the appearance of the town, but the metal which it contained!

My two friends and I, purposing to remain there only a night, had no sooner arrived, than word had flown it seems through the town that a strange poetical chap had arrived there, and a deputation was sent to us, inviting us to a supper at the Tontine Hotel. Of course we accepted; and, on going there, found no fewer than thirty gentlemen assembled to welcome us, and among the rest was Mr. Galt, then a tall thin young man, with something a little dandyish in his appearance. He was dressed in a frock-coat and new top-boots; and it being then the fashion to wear the shirt collars as high as the eyes, Galt wore his the whole of that night with the one side considerably above his ear, and the other flapped over the collar of his frock-coat down to his shoulder. He had another peculiarity, which appeared to me a singular instance of perversity. He walked with his spectacles on, and conversed with them on; but when he read he took them off. In short, from his first appearance, one would scarcely have guessed him to be a man of genius.

The first thing that drew my attention to him was an argument about the moral tendency of some of Shakspeare's plays, in which, though he had two opponents, and one of them both obstinate and loquacious, he managed his part with such good-nature and such strong emphatic reasoning, that my heart whispered me again and again, "This is no common youth." Then his stories of old-fashioned and odd people were so infinitely amusing, that his conversation proved one of the principal charms of that enchanting night. The conversation of that literary community of friends at Greenock, as well as their songs and stories, was much above what I had ever been accustomed to hear. I formed one other intimate and highly valued acquaintance that night, which continued with increasing affection till his lamented death: I allude to James Park, Esq., junior, of that place, Mr. Galt's firm and undeviating friend. I like Galt's writings exceedingly, and have always regretted that he has depicted so much that is selfish and cunning in the Scottish character, and so little that is truly amiable, when he could have done it so well. Of my literary acquaintances in London I dare not say a word until I get back to my native mountains again, when I expect that my reminiscences of them will form a theme of great delight.

LOCKHART

When it is considered what literary celebrity Lockhart has gained so early in life, and how warm and disinterested a friend he has been to me, it argues but little for my sagacity that I scarcely recollect any thing of our first encounters. He was a mischievous Oxford puppy, for whom I was terrified, dancing after the young ladies, and drawing caricatures of every one who came in contact with him. But then I found him constantly in company with all the better rank of people with whom I associated, and consequently it was impossible for me not to meet with him. I dreaded his eye terribly; and it was not without reason, for he was very fond of playing tricks on me, but always in such a way, that it was impossible to lose temper with him. I never parted company with him that my judgment was not entirely jumbled with regard to characters, books, and literary articles of every description. Even his household economy seemed clouded in mystery; and if I got any explanation, it was sure not to be the right thing. It may be guessed how astonished I was one day, on perceiving six black servants waiting at his table upon six white gentlemen! Such a train of Blackamoors being beyond my comprehension, I asked for an explanation; but got none, save that he found them very useful and obliging poor fellows, and that they did not look for much wages, beyond a mouthful of meat.

A young lady hearing me afterwards making a fuss about such a phenomenon, and swearing that the Blackamoors would break my young friend, she assured me that Mr. Lockhart had only *one* black servant, but that when the master gave a dinner to his friends, the servant, knowing there would be enough, and to spare, for all, invited his friends also. Lockhart always kept a good table, and a capital stock of liquor, especially Jamaica rum, and by degrees I grew not so frightened to visit him.

After Wilson and he, and Sym and I had resolved on supporting Blackwood, it occasioned us to be oftener together; but Lockhart contrived to keep my mind in the utmost perplexity for years, on all things that related to that Magazine. Being often curious to know when the tremendous articles appeared who were the authors, and being sure I could draw nothing out of either Wilson, or Sym, I always repaired to Lockhart to ask him, awaiting his reply with fixed eyes and a beating heart. Then, with his cigar in his mouth, his one leg flung carelessly over the other, and without the symptom of a smile on his face, or one twinkle of mischief in his dark grey eye, he would father the articles on his brother, Captain Lockhart, or Peter Robertson, or Sheriff Cay, or James Wilson, or that queer fat body, Dr. Scott; and sometimes on James and John Ballantyne, and Sam Anderson, and poor Baxter. Then away I flew with the wonderful news to my other associates; and if any remained incredulous, I swore the facts down through them; so that before I left Edinburgh I was accounted the greatest liar that was in it, except one. I remember once, at a festival of the Dilletanti Society, that Lockhart was sitting next me, and charming my ear with some story of authorship. I have forgot what it was; but think it was about somebody reviewing his own book. On which I said the incident was such a capital one, that I would give a crown bowl of punch to ascertain if it were true.

"What?" said Bridges; "did any body ever hear the like of that? I hope you are not suspecting your young friend of telling you a falsehood?"

"Haud your tongue Davie, for ye ken naething about it," said I.

"Could ye believe it, man, that that callant never tauld me the truth a' his days but aince, an' that was merely by chance, an' without the least intention on his part?" These blunt accusations diverted Lockhart greatly, and only encouraged him to farther tricks.

I soon found out that the coterie of my literary associates had made it up to act on O'Dogherty's principle, never to deny a thing that they had *not* written, and never to acknowledge one that they *had*. On which I determined that, in future, I would sign my name or designation to every thing I published, that I might be answerable to the world only for my own offences. But as soon as the rascals perceived this, they signed my name as fast as I did. They then contrived the incomparable "Noctes Ambrosianæ," for the sole purpose of putting all the sentiments into the Shepherd's mouth, which they durst not avowedly say themselves, and those too often applying to my best friends. The generality of mankind have always used me ill till I came to London.

The thing that most endeared Lockhart to me at that early period was some humorous poetry which he published anonymously in Blackwood's Magazine, and which I still regard as the best of the same description in the kingdom. He at length married on the same day with myself,[40] into the house of my great friend and patron, and thenceforward I regarded him as belonging to the same family with me, I a step-son, and he a legitimate younger brother.

Of all the practical jokes that ever Lockhart played off on the public in his thoughtless days, the most successful and ludicrous was that about Dr. Scott. He was a strange-looking, bald-headed, bluff little man, that practised as a dentist, both in Glasgow and Edinburgh, keeping a good house and hospitable table in both, and considered skilful; but for utter ignorance of every thing literary, he was not to be matched among a dozen street porters with ropes round their necks. This droll old tippling sinner was a joker in his way, and to Lockhart and his friends a subject of constant mystifications and quizzes, which he partly saw through; but his uncommon vanity made him like the notice, and when at last the wags began to publish songs and ballads in his name, O then he could not resist going into the delusion! and though he had a horrid bad voice, and hardly any ear, he would roar and sing the songs in every company as his own.

[40] Lockhart married Scott's daughter Sophia on 29 April 1820. Hogg's marriage had in fact been on the previous day, 28 April 1820.

Ignorant and uneducated as he was, Lockhart sucked his brains so cleverly, and crammed "The Odontist's" songs with so many of the creature's own peculiar phrases, and the names and histories of his obscure associates, that, though I believe the man could scarce spell a note of three lines, even his intimate acquaintances were obliged to swallow the hoax, and by degrees "The Odontist" passed for a first-rate convivial bard, that had continued to eat and drink and draw teeth for fifty years, and more, without ever letting the smallest corner of the napkin appear to be lifted, under which his wonderful talents had lain concealed.[41] I suspect Captain Tom Hamilton,[42] the original O'Dogherty, had also some hand in that ploy; at least he seemed to enjoy it as if he had, for though he pretended to be a high and starched Whig, he was always engaged with these madcap Tories, and the foremost in many of their wicked contrivances.

Well, at last this joke took so well, and went so far, that shortly after the appearance of "The Lament for Captain Patton," one of John Lockhart's best things, by-the-bye, but which was published in the doctor's name, he happened to take a trip to Liverpool in a steam-boat, and had no sooner arrived there than he was recognised and hailed as Ebony's glorious Odontist! The literary gentry got up a public dinner for him in honour of his great and versatile genius, and the body very coolly accepted the compliment, replying to the toasts and speeches, and all the rest of it. And what is more, none of them ever found him out; which to me, who knew him so well, was quite wonderful. What would I have given to have been at that meeting! I am sure Dean Swift himself never played off a more successful hit than this of "The Odontist."

He is long since dead; but he left a name behind him which has continued to this day, when I have let the secret out. Had he lived till now, I am persuaded his works would have swelled out to volumes, and would have been published in his name, with his portrait at the beginning. I never heard whether he left Lockhart any legacy or not; but he certainly ought to have done so, and both to him and Captain Hamilton. Even the acute Johnie Ballantyne was entrapped,

[41] Further information on the affair of the "Odontist" is given in Mrs Oliphant, *Annals of a Publishing House: William Blackwood and his Sons* (Edinburgh and London, 1897), vol. I, p. 211–13.

[42] Thomas Hamilton (1789–1842), friend of Lockhart, settled in Edinburgh c. 1818 and became one of the Blackwood group. He lived for a time at Chiefswood after Lockhart moved to London: Scott found him a congenial neighbour.

and requested me several times to bring him acquainted with that Dr. Scott, who was one of the most original and extraordinary fellows he had ever met with in print, and he wished much to have the honour of being his publisher. In answer to this request I could only laugh in the bibliopole's face, having been for that once in the true secret. I could tell several stories fully as good as this; but as John is now a reformed character, to all appearance, I shall spare him for the present. Wilson's and his merry doings of those days would make a singular book, and perhaps I may attempt to detail them before I die.

SYM

I first met with that noble and genuine old Tory, the renowned Timothy Tickler,[43] in his own hospitable mansion of South Side, *alias* George's Square, in the south corner of Edinburgh, and to which I was introduced by one of his sister's sons, I think Mr. Robert Wilson, the professor's second brother.

At the very first appearance of my weekly paper "The Spy," Mr. Sym interested himself for it. Not only did his name appear first on the list of subscribers, but he recommended it strongly to all his friends and acquaintances, as a paper worthy of being patronised. Some of the fine madams pointed out to him a few inadvertences, or more properly absurdities, which had occurred in the papers; but he replied, "O, I don't deny that; but I like them the better for these, as they show me at once the character of the writer. I believe him to be a very great blockhead; still I maintain, that there is some smeddum[44] in him."

As the paper went on, he sent me some written advices anonymously, which were excellent, and which I tried to conform to as much as I could. He also sent me some very clever papers for the work, which appeared in it, but all the while kept himself closely concealed from me. It is natural to suppose that I had the most kindly feeling towards this friendly stranger; but it was not till I became acquainted with the Wilsons long afterwards that I knew who he was. When Mr Robert informed me that he was his uncle, I was all impatience to see him.

A little while before the conclusion of "The Spy," Mr. Aikman,

[43] Sym's name in the *Noctes Ambrosianae*. He was the uncle of Professor John Wilson, "Christopher North".

[44] *smeddum* mettle, spirit, force of character, sagacity.

G

the publisher, told me one day that he suspected the friend who had interested himself so much in my success was a Mr. Sym; but I had never heard more than merely his name, and imagined him to be some very little man about Leith. Judge of my astonishment, when I was admitted by a triple-bolted door into a grand house in George's Square, and introduced to its lord, an uncommonly fine-looking elderly gentleman, about seven feet high, and as straight as an arrow! His hair was whitish, his complexion had the freshness and ruddiness of youth, his looks and address full of kindness and benevolence; but whenever he stood straight up, (for he had always to stoop about half way when speaking to a common-sized man like me,) then you could not help perceiving a little of the haughty air of the determined and independent old aristocrat.

From that time forward, during my stay in Edinburgh, Mr Sym's hospitable mansion was the great evening resort of his three nephews and me; sometimes there were a few friends beside, of whom Lockhart and Samuel Anderson were mostly two; but we four for certain; and there are no jovial evenings of my by-past life which I reflect on with greater delight than those. Tickler is completely an original, as any man may see who has attended to his remarks; for there is no sophistry there, they are every one his own. Nay, I don't believe that North has, would, or durst put a single sentence into his mouth that had not proceeded out of it. No, no; although I was made a scape-goat, no one, and far less a nephew, might do so with Timothy Tickler. His reading, both ancient and modern, is boundless, his taste and perception acute beyond those of other men; his satire keen and biting; but at the same time his good-humour is altogether inexhaustible, save when ignited by coming in collision with Whig or Radical principles. Still there being no danger of that with me, he and I never differed in one single sentiment in our lives, excepting on the comparative merits of some Strathspey reels.

But the pleasantest part of our fellowship is yet to describe. At a certain period of the night our entertainer knew by the longing looks which I cast to a beloved corner of the dining-room what was wanting. Then, with "O, I beg your pardon, Hogg, I was forgetting," he would take out a small gold key that hung by a chain of the same precious metal to a particular button-hole, and stalk away as tall as the life, open two splendid fiddle cases, and produce their contents, first the one, and then the other; but always keeping the best to himself. I'll never forget with what elated dignity he stood straight up in the middle of that floor and rosined his bow: there was a twist of the lip, and an upward beam of the eye, that were truly sublime. Then down we sat side by side, and began—at first gently, and with easy motion, like skilful grooms, keeping ourselves up for the final heat, which was slowly but surely approaching. At the end of every tune we took a glass, and still our enthusiastic admiration of the Scottish tunes increased—our energies of execution redoubled, till, ultimately, it became not only a complete and well-contested race, but a trial of strength to determine which should drown the other. The only feelings short of ecstasy, that came across us in these enraptured moments, were caused by hearing the laugh and joke going on with our friends, as if no such thrilling strains had been flowing. But if Sym's eye chanced at all to fall on them, it instantly retreated upwards again in mild indignation. To his honour be it mentioned, he has left me a legacy of that inestimable violin, provided that I outlive him. But not for a thousand such would I part with my old friend.

COMMENTARY

THE first four notes of the Commentary reprint sections of the 1807 *Memoir* which Hogg omitted in the 1832 *Altrive Tales*. As in the main text, significant variations between the 1807 and 1821 editions are recorded in footnotes.

p. 10. The passage in 07 reads:

The first thing that ever I attempted, was a poetical epistle to a student of divinity, an acquaintance of mine. It was a piece of most fulsome flattery, and was mostly composed of borrowed lines and sentences from Dryden's Virgil, and Harvey's Life of Bruce. I scarcely remember one line of it.

But the first thing that ever I composed that was really my own, was a rhyme, entitled, *An Address to the Duke of Buccleuch, in beha'f o' mysel', an' ither poor fo'k.*

In the same year, after a deal of pains, I finished a song, called, *The Way that the World goes on*; and *Wattie and Geordie'[s] Foreign Intelligence*, an eclogue: These were my first year's productions;[1] and having continued to write on ever since, often without either rhyme or reason, my pieces have multiplied exceedingly. Being little conversant in books, and far less in men and manners, the local circumstances on which some of my pieces are founded, may not be unentertaining to you. It was from a conversation that I had with an old woman, from Lochaber, of the name of Cameron, on which I founded the story of *Glengyle*, a ballad; and likewise the ground-plot of *The Happy Swains*, a pastoral, in four parts. This, which I suppose you have never seen,[2] is a dramatic piece of great length, full of trifles and blunders: part of the latter were owing to my old woman, on whose word I depended, and who must have been as ignorant of the leading incidents of the year 1746 as I was.

In 1795, I began *The Scotch Gentleman*, a comedy, in five long acts; after having been summoned to Selkirk, as a witness against some persons suspected of fishing in close-time. This piece (part of which you have seen) is, in fact, full of faults;[3] yet, on reading it to an Ettrick audience, which I have several times done, it never fails to produce the

[1] In 21 Hogg adds after *productions*: "and in all respects miserably bad".

[2] *seen* 21 has "read".

[3] 21 has: "This piece, which you have seen, is, like all the rest, full of faults;".

most extraordinary convulsions of laughter, besides considerable anxiety.[4] The whole of the third act is taken up with the examination of the fishers; and many of the questions asked, and answers given in court, literally copied.

p. 15. The passage in 07 reads:

It was while confined to my bed from the effects of this dreadful malady that I composed the song, beginning, *Fareweel, ye Grots; fareweel, ye Glens.*

In the year 1800, I began and finished the two first acts of a tragedy, denominated, *The Castle in the Wood*; and, flattering myself that it was about to be a masterpiece, I showed it to Mr William Laidlaw, my literary confessor; who, on returning it, declared it faulty in the extreme; and perceiving that he had black strokes drawn down through several of my most elaborate speeches, I cursed his stupidity, threw it away, and never added another line. My acquaintances hereabouts imagine, that the pastoral of *Willie an' Keatie*, published with others in 1801, was founded on an amour of mine own. I cannot say that their surmises are entirely groundless. The publication of this pamphlet was one of the most unadvised actions that ever was committed.

21 as 07.

p. 16. The passage in 07 reads:

"Willie and Keatie," however, had the honour of being copied into some periodical publications of the time, as "no unfavourable specimen of the work," although, in my opinion, the succeeding one was greatly its superior.[5] In 1802, *The Minstrelsy of the Scottish Border* came into my hands; and, though I was even astonished to find such exact copies of many old songs, which I had heard sung by people who never could read a song, but had them handed down by tradition; and likewise at the conformity of the notes, to the traditions and superstitions which are, even to this day, far from being eradicated from the minds of the people amongst our mountains,—yet, I confess, that I was not satisfied with many of the imitations of the ancients. I immediately chose a number of traditional facts, and set about imitating the different manners of the ancients myself. The chief of these are, *The Death of Douglas, Lord of Liddesdale, The Heir of Thirlestane, Sir David Graham, The*

[4] *besides considerable anxiety* Not in 21, which has instead: "though I was sometimes afraid that the laugh was rather at *me* than at the circumstances of the plot".

[5] After *superior* 21 has an extra sentence: "Indeed, all of them were sad stuff, although I judged them to be exceedingly good."

Pedlar, and *John Scott of Harden*, by the Scotts of Gilmanscleuch.[6] The only other local circumstance on which any other of my pieces is founded, was the following:—In 1801, I went to Edinburgh on foot, and being benighted at Straiton, lodged there, where the landlord had a son deranged in his mind, whom his father described as having been formerly sensible and docile. His behaviour was very extravagant; he went out at night, and attacked the moon with great rudeness and vociferation. I was so taken with his condition, that I tarried another night on my way home, to contemplate his manner and ideas a little farther.

Thinking that a person in such a state, with a proper cause assigned, was a fit subject for a poem,—before I reached home, I had all the incidents arranged, and a good many verses composed, of the pastoral tale of *Sandy Tod*. I think it one of the best of my tender[7] pieces. Most of my prose essays have been written in an epistolary form. You may have seen, by the papers, that I gained two premiums from the Highland Society, for essays connected with the rearing and management of sheep. I have gone three journies into the Highlands; two on foot, and one on horseback; at each time penetrating farther, until I have seen a great part of that rough, but valuable country. I have copied out the most of my journals into letters for your perusal, and will proceed with the rest at my leisure: who knows but you may one day think of laying them before the public?[8] I have always had a great partiality for the Highlands of Scotland, and now intend going to settle in one of its most distant corners. The issue of such an adventure, time only can reveal.

p. 17. The passage in 07 reads:

This transaction did not savour with my countrymen; they looked on me as a fugitive, and railed at me without mercy; though why, or for what reason, I have never been able to comprehend, as the only person who had even the least prospect of losing by it, always stood my firm friend. It, however, gave me the opportunity of learning exactly who were really my friends; a knowledge which is of greater consequence than many are aware.

I am, &c.
JAMES HOGG.

21 as in *Altrive Tales* text. 07 ends at this point.

[6] This sentence is not in 21, which has instead: "These ballads you have seen; and as they are the first things which you have approved, I have some thoughts of intruding myself once more on the public."

[7] *tender* 21 has "early".

[8] *who knows . . . public?* Omitted in 21.

p. 21. Hogg's *Memoir* was attacked in 1832 by Dr James Browne in a pamphlet, *The "Life" of the Ettrick Shepherd anatomized . . . by an old dissector*. The motive behind this pamphlet appears to be party political feeling; it is a Whig attack on Hogg and his Tory associates. It does however contain evidence which indicates that Hogg's account in the *Memoir* of his dealings with Messrs Aikman over *The Spy* is somewhat disingenuous:

Now, to enable the reader to judge for himself of Hogg's talent for relating "the downright truth," we shall here insert an excerpt from a statement with which we have been favoured respecting this matter, by Mr Andrew Aikman, formerly a partner of the firm of A. and J. Aikman, proprietors of the Star newspaper. This statement, which is holograph of Mr Aikman, subscribed by him, and dated the 2d of May 1832, is as follows:—

After some introductory remarks, and quoting Hogg's words above cited, Mr Aikman proceeds: "Mr Hogg, in the above, has given the truth, *but not all the truth*. It shall now be stated. When Mr Hogg first applied to A. and J. Aikman, he brought Mr Grieve, and another gentleman whose name is now forgotten, with him, and produced his list of subscribers, booksellers and others, which *appeared* sufficiently respectable to induce them to undertake the publication on the terms he states, with this additional provision, that as they were to be at all the outlay, so they were to receive *all* the subscriptions; and when the work was finished, then accounts were to be balanced, and the profits divided. But Mr Hogg has not fairly stated this matter: he has not said that he gave to them a list of subscribers, *principally booksellers*, who, with the exception of Mr John Ballantyne, *were merely agents*, and who had the work, according to the technical phrase, *on sale and return*; and from Glasgow, Greenock, &c., they were out of pocket by carriages, *from the most of the numbers being returned to them*; and when Mr Ballantyne was applied to, whose name was put down for *fifty* copies, he refused to pay or return the copies, Mr Hogg being much more than the amount in his debt.

"Another part of Mr Hogg's unfair dealing was this:—He knew that immediately after the publication of the 4th number (which, it was reported, was a *sketch* of his own *life* up to the time of his coming to Edinburgh—*and a more shameful and indecent paper was never laid so barefacedly before the public*, but which, however, had been cancelled) the subscribers had decreased amazingly. This, however, he *kept secret* from A. and J. Aikman till after they were so engaged that they could not draw back: they, therefore, went on and finished the work; but it was not till that period that they knew of the extent of the loss to which they had subjected themselves. It is said above, that A. and J. Aikman were to be the *sole receivers* of the subscriptions; but it unfortunately turned out that Mr Hogg acted with *as little faith* in this as in other parts of his engagement; for, on application to many of the subscribers, *it was found he* [Hogg] HAD RECEIVED THE MONEY; and even his friend Mr ——'s subscription is not paid to this day.

"With respect to their not rendering an exact account of their concern in the transaction, *that is utterly false*; they rendered this at the time when Mr Hogg was proposing to make a composition with his creditors; and for his share of the loss they were to receive *ten shillings* in the pound, which, however, has never been forthcoming; so that A. and J. Aikman, with the exception of about eighteen pounds, which they collected during the course of the publication, *lost every thing else.*

"It may just be mentioned in conclusion, that, happening to meet casually with Mr Hogg in Argyle Square a good many months ago, I [Mr A. Aikman] taxed him with what he had said of A. and J. Aikman in his first edition, when *he denied all recollection of it*, and said *he never* INTENDED *to have advanced anything to the detriment of our characters.* How he has allowed himself to reprint the same I know not; but it either shows the height of malice or the extreme of folly. I was much pressed at the time he published his first edition to contradict his statement; but I really cared little about the slanders of a man who could allow his name to make such a conspicuous figure in the *Noctes Ambrosianæ.*"

(Signed)   "ANDREW AIKMAN."

p. 25. Goldie attacked Hogg's *Memoir* vigorously in a pamphlet, *Letter to a Friend*, which was published after the 1821 and 1832 printings of the *Memoir*. Goldie's most important charges are contained in the following passage, which refers to his bankruptcy, and to the preceding publication of the third edition of *The Queen's Wake* (*Memoir*, p. 27–8):

The first assertion, that "a third edition" was wanted, is not true,— even a second edition was not called for; but Mr Hogg represented it as "the third" to Mr Constable, which, together with other statements equally untrue, respecting my declining again putting it to the press, he succeeded in persuading Mr Constable to engage in the publication; but Mr Hogg's falsehood being subsequently seen through by Mr Constable, that gentleman declined proceeding any farther in the business; and, in as far as I have ever been able to learn, Mr Constable has had no more connexion with Mr Hogg from that day to this! For the truth of this I confidently refer to Mr Constable himself.

As to the edition not being lodged in my premises a week before I stopped, it is unfortunate for Mr Hogg, that, by a comparison of dates, he will find this week to have been several months! For the truth of this, *vide* Mr Bridges and the printer!

Of the next charge, which implies a crime of the greatest magnitude, and which is punishable by the highest penalties of the law,—that of clandestinely disposing of property when on the eve of bankruptcy— I can only say, that my affairs were carefully examined by Mr Francis Bridges, Mr Blackwood, and Mr Samuel Aiken, persons in every respect qualified for such a task; and I call upon these gentlemen, one and all of them, to say, if, in the course of their duty as trustees on my estate, or in any manner whatsoever, they discovered any,—even the LEAST APPEARANCE of a fraudulent act on my part; or in any way heard an insinuation to that effect, until the publication of Mr Hogg's Memoir? The fact is, that, in the certificate, or discharge, which was afterwards granted by my creditors, on the recommendation of these gentlemen, the very contrary is stated, and what is perhaps more extraordinary, Mr Hogg's signature is appended to that document, and now in my possession!

It is true that Goldie's so-called "second" edition of the *Queen's Wake* (1813) was a reissue of the first (also 1813). Goldie's "third" edition (in fact the second) was published in 1814. Constable, however, did act as Hogg's publisher after 1814; he published Hogg's *Poetical Works* in four volumes in 1822.

Hogg says that Goldie, before his bankruptcy, "contrived to sell, or give away, more than half the copies" of the "third" edition. This does not perhaps amount to an unmistakable accusation that Goldie was guilty of "clandestinely disposing of property when on the eve of bankruptcy". However, Hogg no doubt exaggerates the brevity of the time between the publication of the edition and Goldie's bankruptcy.

In another passage Goldie writes:

Mr Hogg says, "before this time, one George Goldie, a young bookseller in Princes' Street, a lad of SOME TASTE, had become acquainted with me at the Forum, and earnestly requested to see my MS." (that is the MS. of the Queen's Wake.) This statement, simple as it is, is quite inaccurate. I did NOT become acquainted with him at the Forum; on the contrary, HE WAITED ON ME, because, as he said, Mr Constable had refused to publish for him. This declaration of his was accompanied with observations on Mr Constable's behaviour to him, too coarse and vulgar to be repeated, and which, I believe, were wholly false. With regard to his offensive commendation of my taste, I can assure Mr Hogg that I am not solicitous of his approbation in that particular.

That is, Hogg turned to Goldie after Constable had refused to publish the *Wake*, because of Constable's refusal. This is disproved, however, by the following letter from Hogg to Constable, which is dated 24 September 1812:

Dear Sir,—Having now completed the Queen's Wake I must settle about the publication, for I am desirous that it should appear in Janr. or Febr. next. Of course, as your right, I give you the first offer of it. My terms are decisively as follows. . . . Geo. Goldie requests a share of it; that shall be as you please. I will expect an answer with your convenience.—I am your obliged   James Hogg.

(Quoted in T. Constable, *Archibald Constable and his literary correspondents*, vol. 2 (1873), p. 355)

That is, Goldie had expressed an interest in the Wake before it was offered to Constable or any other publisher.

Goldie also disputes Hogg's account of his experiences as secretary of the Forum:

Mr Hogg was appointed secretary, and as a matter of CHARITY, had a salary appropriated to him of £20 per annum. None of the office-bearers excepting himself, had one farthing for all their exertions and attendance; but Mr Hogg, with a propensity to falsehood, and a meanness of soul quite inexplicable, gravely and deliberately asserts in page 37 of his Memoirs: "I was appointed secretary, with a salary of £20 a-year, which was never paid, though I gave away hundreds in charity." Now, the simple truth is this—Mr Hogg did receive one year's salary, and a part of the second year's likewise, and he was only not paid the second in full, because the Forum was in debt, and broke up before it was due, when the members were severally called upon to contribute their quota, about £4 or £5, in paying off all claims, which was very generally paid by the individuals, although Mr Hogg formed an exception. He says, "he gave away hundreds in charity." The fact is this, he never gave away one penny! never was intrusted with one penny, or the disposal of a farthing of the funds of the Forum.—It is true, that he once applied, agreeably to the prescribed rules of the society, for a sum of £10, which he alleged was for the use of some poor family that had come under his notice; but such was the distrust of his coadjutors, that this was refused, —unless another party accompanied Mr Hogg in giving away the money. Mr Hogg prudently declined this, and so the matter ended! I never was a member of the Forum, nor had I ever any connexion with it as a collective body, although many individuals composing it were my friends; and I take the liberty of stating these circumstances in justice to them, and I appeal for the truth of what I now say to the Reverend J. Geddes, Paisley, the Reverend Mr Brand, Dunfermline, Mr John M'Diarmid, Dumfries, and many more who know all the circumstances accurately.

Hogg's feelings about Goldie's pamphlet can be gathered from a letter written to Oliver & Boyd, the publishers of the 1821 *Memoir*. The letter is now in the Oliver & Boyd papers in the National Library of Scotland.

> Altrive Lake June 24th 1821
> I'll see the firm of Oliver & Boyd and the dog Goldie d——d to hell before I suffer a syllable of aught I have ever published to be altered. I have a prosecution for a libel out against him already let him look to himself and to me; with you he has nothing to do
>
> James Hogg

Hogg did not in fact proceed with the libel action.
Near the beginning of his pamphlet Goldie writes:

> I may here premise, however, and I beg you will never lose sight of the fact,—as it furnishes a key to all that is to follow,—that when I left Edinburgh, two years ago, it was for the purpose of proceeding to the theatre of war in South America. I have not corresponded with Mr Hogg since, and he actually heard, or supposed I was dead, for when the offensive passages in his work were challenged by a mutual friend as false, Mr Hogg replied, if not in the exact words, at least to the following effect, viz. "I am sorry I should have said any thing against Goldie, but I understood he was dead in South America, or would never more be heard of, and consequently any thing I said would not hurt him!" This anecdote fully illustrates the base intentions of the man. His cowardice suggested, that it was safer to utter calumnies against a dead man, than to insult the feelings of a living one; and, in the belief that I was fairly disposed of, thought it no harm to load my memory with infamy, and inflict an eternal wound upon the feelings of my surviving relations, who may have been supposed incapable of effectually rescuing my name from so foul a stain. I have this story from Mr John Grieve, who is the mutual friend above alluded to, and the person to whom Mr Hogg dedicates one of his poems, of whose candour and veracity there can be no question.

Goldie's flyting is spirited, but another interpretation of Hogg's words as reported here is perhaps possible. Hogg is quoted as saying

"I understood he was dead . . . and consequently anything I said would not hurt him"; perhaps this means simply that Hogg would not have said anything to hurt Goldie's commercial career had he thought Goldie was still alive. If cowardice *was* his motive, it is difficult to see why he reprinted his account of his dealings with Goldie in 1832.

p. 38. The project which culminated in *The Poetic Mirror* began as a scheme for a half-yearly "poetical repository", the nature of which Hogg explained in a letter to Byron of 3 June 1814:

> I suppose it is not uncommon for minor bards to ask and expect favours from those who are their superiors in reputation and fortune, but in general they will ask many things before they ask *poetry* yet of all others that is the very thing I request of your lordship. To be explicit there has been a little plan suggested by a few literary and benevolent gentlemen for the behalf of an humble son of song. It is to establish a poetical repository in Edin. to be continued half-yearly part of it to consist of original poetry and the remainder to be filled up with short reviews or characters of every poetical work published in the interim and in order to give it currency at first and secure subscribers to a certain requisite amount we are desirous of procuring something original from every great poet in Britain for the early numbers at least Roscoe Southey Scott Wordsworth Wilson and many others of high respect have already assented. I have long been wriggling with this and that friend to procure me a promise of something from you till the other day happening to mention it to Scott he told me in what warm and impressive terms you have mentioned me in some letters to him, and said that he was sure you would attend to myself sooner than to any that could apply for me which induced me to use this liberty with your lordship.

This letter is quoted in A. L. Strout, *Life and Letters of James Hogg* (1946), p. 73.

Hogg again mentions the project in a letter to Byron of 11 October 1814 (Strout p. 86–7):

> But I have the far worst thing of all to relate, and which in my own eyes crowns my misfortunes, and upon the whole renders my situation so whimsical that I cannot help laughing at it, for nothing of that nature makes me cry. *I have differed with Scott*, actually and seriously I fear, for I hear he has informed some of his friends of it. I have often heard poets in general blamed for want of common sense, yet I know that Scott has a great deal of it; but I fear he has had to do with one who had little or none at all.

I have never mentioned this to any living soul, nor would I, if I had not heard last night that Scott had mentioned it in a company, and that it was like to become publicly known. Therefore I must tell you all how it fell out, though I cannot explain it. At our last meeting it was most cordially agreed that he was not to appear in the first No. of the *Repository*, but to exert himself for the second. "The first," said he, "is secured if Lord Byron sends a piece of any length. With those which you already have, I shall take in hand to get you £500 for this number. The difficulty will be in keeping it up, therefore depend on it, I shall do my best to support the second No." All this was very well, till of late we had a correspondence about a drama that I was attempting. He sent a sheet of criticisms in his own shrewd sensible manner and most friendly. But in the last page he broke off and attacked me about some jealousies and comparisons between him and me so cavalierly, that I was driven completely out of myself, and without asking any explanation (for I knew no more than the man in the moon what he adverted to), I took the pen and wrote a letter of the most bitter and severe reproaches. I have quite forgot what in my wrath I said; but I believe I went so far as to say everything which I knew to be the reverse of the truth, and which you in part well know—yea, to state that I had never been obliged to him (it was a great lie) and never would be obliged to him for any thing; and I fear I expressed the utmost contempt for both himself and his poetry! . . .

Thus one of the best props of the *Repository* is irrevocably lost. If the other should likewise prove a bruised reed, why, every herring must hang by its own head. . . .

This clearly gives a different account of the quarrel with Scott from that given in the *Memoir*, and Strout (p.112–13) is inclined to reject the version in the *Memoir* for this reason. But, if the quarrel was about Scott's remarks at the end of his criticism of Hogg's drama as the letter says, then it is difficult to see why Hogg did not say so in the *Memoir*. If, however, the *Memoir* is correct in stating that the quarrel was over Scott's refusal to contribute to the repository, then it is clear that Hogg had strong reasons for concealing this from Byron. Byron would be unlikely to contribute if Scott had refused, and a contribution from either Scott or Byron was essential if the project were to succeed.

FAMILIAR ANECDOTES OF
SIR WALTER SCOTT

IN the following miscellaneous narrative I do not pretend to give a life of my illustrious and regretted friend.[1] That has been done by half-a-dozen already and will ultimately be given by his son in law fully and clearly, the only man who is thoroughly qualified for the task and is in possession of the necessary documents. The whole that I presume to do is after an intimate acquaintance of thirty years to give a few simple and personal anecdotes which no man can give but myself. It is well known what Sir Walter was in his study but these are to show what he was in the parlour in his family and among his acquaintances and in giving them I shall in nothing extenuate or set down aught through partiality and as for malice that is out of the question. (*then copy the whole of the Reminiscences of him in The Altrive Tales*)[2]

The only foible I ever could discover in the character of Sir Walter was a too strong leaning to the old aristocracy of the country. His devotion for titled rank was prodigious and in such an illustrious character altogether out of place. It amounted almost to adoration and not to mention the numerous nobility whom I have met at his own house and in his company I shall give a few instances of that sort of feeling in him to which I allude.

Although he of course acknowledged Buccleuch as the head and chief of the whole clan of Scott yet he always acknowledged Harden as his immediate chieftain and head of that powerful and numerous sept of the name and Sir Walter was wont often to relate how he and his father before him and his grandfather before that always kept their Christmas with Harden in acknowledgment of their vassalage. This he used to tell with a degree of exultation which I always thought must have been astounding to every one who heard it as if his illustrious name did not throw a blaze of glory on the house of

[1] The text is reprinted from Hogg's manuscript (see Introduction). Hogg sometimes omits the full stop at the end of his sentences, and sometimes includes it. When it is clear that a full stop is understood (for example because the next word in the manuscript begins with a capital) it has been supplied. In a few places, indicated by footnotes, additional punctuation has been supplied to avoid obscurity. Otherwise Hogg's punctuation is followed exactly. On one or two occasions a word or phrase has been supplied in square brackets where this seems to be required by the sense.

[2] In the printed versions of the *Familiar Anecdotes* the Reminiscences of Scott from the *Memoir of the Author's Life* (see *Memoir*, p. 61-6) are reprinted at this point, with a number of changes. See Commentary.

H

Harden a hundred times more than that van of old Border barbarians however brave could throw over him.

He was likewise descended from the chiefs of Haliburton and Rutherford on the maternal side and to the circumstance of his descent from these three houses he adverted so often mingling their arms in his escutcheon that to me who alas to this day could never be brought to discern any distinction in ranks save what was constituted by talents or moral worth it appeared perfectly ludicrous thinking as no man could help thinking of the halo which his genius shed over those families while he only valued himself as a descendant of theirs.

I may mention one other instance at which I was both pleased and mortified. We chanced to meet at a great festival at Bowhill[3] when Duke Charles was living and in good health. The company being very numerous there were two tables set in the dining room one along and one across. They were nearly of the same length but at the one along the middle of the room all the ladies were seated mixed alternately with gentlemen and at this table all were noble save if I remember aright Sir Adam Ferguson[4] whose everlasting good humour insures him a passport into every company. But I having had some chat with the ladies before dinner and always rather a flattered pet with them imagined they could not possibly live without me and placed myself among them. But I had a friend at the cross table at the head of the room who saw better. Sir Walter who presided there arose and addressing the Duke of Buccleuch requested of him as a particular favour and obligation that he would allow Mr Hogg to come to his table for that in fact he could not do without him and moreover he added

> If ye reave the Hoggs o Fauldshope
> Ye herry Harden's gear

I of course got permission and retired to Sir Walter's table where he placed me on the right hand of the gentleman on his right hand who of course was Scott of Harden.[5] And yet notwithstand[ing] the broad

[3] The seat of the Buccleuch family.

[4] Sir Adam Ferguson (1771–1855), keeper of the regalia in Scotland, the son of Adam Ferguson the philosopher, and Scott's life-long friend.

[5] Lockhart comments on this passage as follows (*Memoirs of the Life of Sir Walter Scott* (1837), vol. 3, p. 398): "It is a pity that I should have occasion to allude, before I quit a scene so characteristic of Scott, to another outbreak of Hogg's jealous humour. His Autobiography informs us, that when the more distinguished part of the company

insinuation about the Hoggs of Fauldshope I sat beside that esteemed gentleman the whole night and all the while took him for an English clergyman! I knew there were some two or three clergymen of rank there connected with the family and I took Harden for one of them and though I was mistaken I still say he ought to have been one. I was dumfoundered next day when the Duke told me that my divine whom I thought so much of was Scott of Harden for I would have liked so well to have talked with him about old matters my forefathers having been vassals under that house on the lands of Fauldshope for more than two centuries and were only obliged to change masters with the change of proprietors. It was doubtless owing to this connection that my father had instilled into my youthful mind so many traditions relating to the house of Harden[6] of which I have made considerable use.

But the anecdote which I intended to relate before my ruling passion of egotism came across me was this. When the dinner came to be served Sir Walter refused to let a dish be set on our table[7]

assembled on the conclusion of the sport to dine at Bowhill, he was proceeding to place himself at a particular table—but the Sheriff seized his arm, told him *that* was reserved for the nobility, and seated him at an inferior board—'between himself and the Laird of Harden,'—the first gentleman of the clan Scott. 'The fact is,' says Hogg, 'I am convinced he was sore afraid of my getting to be too great a favourite among the young ladies of Buccleuch!' Who can read this, and not be reminded of Sancho Panza and the Duchess? And, after all, he quite mistook what Scott had said to him; for certainly there was, neither on this, nor any similar occasion at Bowhill, any *high table for the nobility*, though there was a *side-table for the children*, at which, when the Shepherd of Ettrick was about to seat himself, his friend probably whispered that it was reserved for the '*little* lords and ladies, and their playmates'. This blunder may seem undeserving of any explanation; but it is often in small matters that the strongest feelings are most strikingly betrayed—and this story is, in exact proportion to its silliness, indicative of the jealous feeling which mars and distorts so many of Hogg's representations of Scott's conduct and demeanour." Lockhart was presumably describing Hogg's account from memory, as he mistakenly states it appears in the "Autobiography". A comparison of Lockhart's description of Hogg's anecdote with what Hogg actually wrote reveals a remarkable degree of distortion and unfairness to Hogg. Lockhart dates this incident in 1815, three years before he himself first met Scott.

[6] Hogg's manuscript has "harden".

[7] In the *Domestic Manners*, the 1834 British reprint of the *Familiar Anecdotes*, a number of footnotes were added to the text. At this point the following footnote appears: "Sir Walter, practical, and with a strong grasp of real life in his poetry, was always endeavouring to live in a world of fiction. His Abbotsford, the dinner here narrated, and the reception of the king at Edinburgh were continuous efforts to transplant himself into another age—not unlike children playing Crusaders, Reavers, Robinson Crusoes, &c."

Some of the *Domestic Manners* footnotes are tactless and offensive. While it is clear that some of them are not by Hogg (one reads "Saul among the prophets! Hogg quoting

which had not been first presented to the Duke and the nobility. "No no! said he "This is literally a meeting of the Clan and its adherents and we shall have one dinner in the feudal stile. It may be but for once in our lives."

As soon as the Duke perceived this whim he admitted of it although I believe the dishes were merely set down and lifted again. In the mean time the venison and beef stood on the side board which was free to all so that we were all alike busy from the beginning.

At the end of our libations and before we parted some time in the course of the morning the Duke set his one foot on the table and the other on his chair requesting us all to do the same with which every man complied and in that position he sung "Johnie Cope are ye wauking yet" while all joined in the chorus. Sir Walter set his weak foot on the table and kept his position steadily apparently more firm than when he stood on the floor joining in the chorus with his straight forward bass voice[8] with great glee and enjoying the whole scene exceedingly as he did every scene of hilarity that I ever saw. But though a more social companion never was born he never filled himself drunk. He took always his wine after dinner and at least for upwards of twenty years a little gin toddy after supper but he was uniformly moderate in eating and drinking. He liked a good breakfast but often confessed that he never knew what a good breakfast was till he came to my cottage but he should never want it again and he kept steadily to his resolution.

He was a most extraordinary being. How or when he composed his voluminous works no man could tell. When in Edin[r] he was bound to the parliament house all the forenoon. He never was denied to any living neither lady or gentleman poor nor rich and he never

---

Latin!"), it has been suggested that he may have been responsible for the others (see, for example, Louis Simpson, *James Hogg: a Critical Study* (1962), p. 46). However, if the argument in the Introduction that the *Domestic Manners* was a pirated edition is valid, then it is clear that Hogg was not responsible for any of these footnotes.

Two footnotes are added in the *Domestic Manners* to the material which is reprinted from the *Memoir* in *Altrive Tales*. The first concerns the description of the leistering— "Sir Walter alludes in the notes to his collected work by Cadell, to his 'fire hunting' expeditions. Hogg enables us to fill up the outline of one of them." The note "Guy Mannering" is also added to the phrase which describes the salmon "turning up sides like swine". See Commentary.

[8] "Which means, we suppose, a voice that never varied its notes; no—
winding bout
Of linked sweetness long drawn out."
—*Domestic Manners.*

seemed discomposed when intruded on but always good humoured and kind. Many a time have I been sorry for him for I have remained in his study in Castle street in hopes to get a quiet word of him and witnessed the admission of ten intruders foreby myself. Noblemen Gentlemen painters poets and players all crowded to Sir Walter not to mention booksellers and printers who were never absent but these spoke to him privately. When at Abbotsford for a number of years his house was almost constantly filled with company for there was a correspondence carried on and always as one freight went away another came. It was impossible not to be sorry for the time of such a man thus broken in upon. I felt it exceedingly and once when I went down by particular invitation to stay a fortnight I had not the heart to stay any longer than three days and that space was generally the length of my visits. But Sir Walter never was discomposed. He was ready as soon as breakfast was over to accompany his guests wherever they chose to go to stroll in the wood or take a drive up to Yarrow or down to Melrose or Dryburgh where his sacred ashes now repose. He was never out of humour when well but when ill he was very cross he being subject to a billious complaint of the most dreadful and severe nature accompanied by pangs most excrutiating,[9] and when under the influence of that malady it was not easy to speak to him and I found it always the best plan to keep a due distance. But then his sufferings had been most intense for he told me one day when he was sitting as yellow as a primrose that roasted salt had been prescribed to lay on the pit of his stomach which was applied and the next day it was discovered that his breast was all in a blister and the bosom of his shirt burnt to an izel[10] and yet he never felt it!

But to return to our feast at Bowhill from which I have strangely wandered although the best of the fun is yet to come. When the Duke retired to the drawing-room he deputed Sir Alex[r] Don who sat next him to his chair. We had long before been all at one table. Sir Alex[r] instantly requested a bumper out of champaign

---

[9] "This fact—which we do not recollect to have seen noticed before, accounts for some inequalities of temper we have heard laid to Sir Walter's charge—his uncourteous treatment of Lord Holland, &c. Before blaming any one for such freaks, we ought always to inquire into the state of the stomach."—*Domestic Manners*. For Scott's "uncourteous treatment of Lord Holland" see Edgar Johnson, *Sir Walter Scott* (1970), p. 331. Descriptions of the pain suffered by Scott during these attacks can be found in Lockhart's *Life*.

[10] *izel* a hot cinder.

glasses to the Duke's health with all the honours. It was instantly complied with and every one drank it to the bottom. Don then proposed the following of so good an example as His Grace had set us and accordingly we were obliged all to mount our chairs again and setting one foot on the table sing Johny Cope over again. Every one at least attempted it and Sir Alex^r sung the song in most capital stile. The Scotts and the Elliotts and some Taits now began to fall with terrible thuds on the floor but Sir Walter still kept his station as steady as a rock and laughed immoderately. But this was too good fun to be given up. The Marquis of Queensberry who was acting as Croupier said that such a loyal and social Border Clan could never separate without singing "God save the King" and that though we had drunk to his health at the beginning we behoved to do it again and join in the Anthem. We were obliged to mount our chairs again and in the same ticklish position sing The King's Anthem. Down we went one after another. Nay they actually fell in heaps above each other. I fell off and took a devil of a run to one corner of the room against which I fell which created great merriment. There was not above six stood the test this time out of from thirty to forty. Sir Walter did and he took all the latter bumpers off to the brim. He had a good head more ways than one.

There was no man who ever testified more admiration and even astonishment than he did at my poetical productions both songs and poems and sometimes in very high terms before his most intimate friends. It was somewhat different with regard to my prose works with which he uniformly found fault and always with the disagreeable adjunction "how good they might have been made with a little pains." When *the Three Perils of Man*[11] was first put to press he requested to see the proof slips Ballantyne having been telling him something about the work. They were sent to him on the instant and on reading them he sent expressly for me as he wanted to see and speak with me about my forthcoming work. We being both at that time residing in Edinb^r I attended directly and I think I remember every word that passed. Indeed so implicit was my dependance on his friendship his good taste and judgement that I never forgot a sentence nor a word that he said to me about my own works but treasured them up in my heart.

"Well Mr Hogg I have read over your proofs with a great deal of pleasure and I confess with some little portion of dread. In the first

[11] Published 1822.

place the meeting of the two princesses at Castle-Weiry is excellent. I have not seen any modern thing more truly dramatic. The characters are all strongly marked old Peter Chisholm's in particular. Ah man what you might have made of that with a little more refinement care and patience! But it is always the same with you just hurrying on from one vagary to another without consistency or proper arrangement."

"Dear Mr Scott a man canna do the thing that he canna do."

"Yes but you *can* do it. Witness your poems where the arrangements are all perfect and complete but in your prose works with the exception of some short tales you seem to write merely by random without once considering what you are going to write about."

"You are not often wrong Mr Scott and you were never righter in your life than you are now for when I write the first line of a tale or novel I know not what the second is to be and it is the same way in every sentence throughout. When my tale is traditionary the work is easy as I then see my way before me though the tradition be ever so short but in all my prose works of imagination knowing little of the world I sail on without star or compass."

"I am sorry to say that is often but too apparent. But in the next place and it was on that account I sent for you. Do you not think there is some little danger in making Sir Walter Scott of Buccleuch the hero of this wild extravagant tale?"

"The devil a bit."

"Well I think differently. The present chief is your patron your sincere friend and your enthusiastic admirer. Would it not then be a subject of regret not only to yourself and me but to all Scotland should you by any rash adventure forfeit the countenance and friendship of so good and so great a man?"[12]

"There's nae fears o' that ata' Mr Scott. The Sir Walter o' my

12 The *Domestic Manners* was reviewed, most unfavourably, by William Maginn in *Fraser's Magazine*, vol. 10 (1834), p. 125–6. Maginn writes: "But see how a few plain dates will put down the story of the *Three Perils of Man*, and the conversation about it above reported. The work appeared in 1822; and we find Hogg addressing Scott as *Mr*. Scott four several times—Sir Walter having been created a baronet in 1820. That may be a slip of memory; but when we find that Sir Walter is made to remonstrate against making his namesake the hero of that silly story, on the ground that it might offend the chief of Buccleuch, the 'great and good man,' who was at that time Hogg's patron, there can be no slip. The father of the present Duke of Buccleuch died in 1819. Hogg therefore could not have been afraid of losing his patronage in 1822. The present Duke of Buccleuch was a lad at school about 17 years of age, who of course could not have been called a great and good man by Sir Walter Scott, and who certainly was not then, nor indeed ever after, the sincere friend and enthusiastic admirer of Hogg. We suppose it is

tale is a complete hero throughout and is never made to do a thing or say a thing of which his descendant our present chief winna be proud."

"I am not quite sure of that do you not think you have made him a rather too selfish character?"

["] Oo ay but ye ken they were a' a little gi'en that gate else how could they hae gotten haud o' a' the South o' Scotland nae body kens how?"

Sir Walter then took to himself a hearty laugh and then pronounced these very words. "Well Hogg you appear to me just now like a man dancing upon a rope or wire at a great height. If he is successful and finishes his dance in safety he has accomplished no great matter but if he makes a slip he gets a devil of a fall."

"Never say another word about it Mr Scott, I'm satisfied, the designation shall be changed throughout before I either eat or sleep, and I kept my word.

I went when in Edinb^r at his particular request two or three days every week to breakfast with him as I was then always sure of an hour's conversation with him before he went to the parliament house and I often went for many days successively and soon found it was impossible to be in his company without gaining advantage. But there was one Sunday morning I found him in very bad humour indeed. He was sitting at his desk in his study at Castle-street and when I went in he looked up to me with a visage as stern as that of a judge going to pronounce sentence on a malefactor and at the same time he neither rose nor saluted me which was always his wont and the first words that he addressed to me were these—"Mr Hogg I am very angry with you. I tell you it plainly; and I think I have a

quite unnecessary, after these two facts, on the correctness of which the truth of the main incident of the conversation turns, to say that the whole is a sheer invention."

One of the leading characters in *The Three Perils of Man* inhabits the ancient Buccleuch stronghold of Mount Comyn, is a blood relation of Michael Scott, and is himself spoken of as a Scott. He is clearly a Scott of Buccleuch, but throughout the book his name appears as Sir Ringan Redhough. Hogg in 1822 had rent-free possession of the Buccleuch farm of Altrive Lake, and there seems no reason to doubt that he changed "Sir Walter" to "Sir Ringan" to avoid offending his patrons. Equally there seems no reason to doubt that he was advised to do so by Scott, or that Scott, in so advising him, reminded him of the gifts and kindness of the late Duke. The dates Maginn quotes therefore prove only that Hogg, muddle-headed as ever about dates, was mistaken in thinking that in 1822 Duke Charles was still alive and Sir Walter was still Mr Scott. As the conversation Hogg records reflects these mistakes it cannot be accurate word for word; nevertheless it seems probable that Hogg accurately records the substance of what was said.

right to be so. I demand sir an explanation of a sentence in your *Spy* of yesterday."

Knowing perfectly well to what sentence he alluded my peasant blood began to boil and I found it rushing to my head and face most violently as I judged myself by far the most aggrieved. "Then I must first demand an explanation from you Mr Scott" said I "Were you the author of the article alluded to in my paper which places you at the head and me at the tail nay as the very dregs of all the poets of Britain?"

"What right had you sir to suppose that I was the author of it" said he in a perfect rage.

"Nay what right had *you* to suppose that you were the author of it that you are taking it so keenly to yourself" said I "The truth is that when I wrote the remarks I neither knew nor cared who was the author of the article alluded to but before the paper went to press I believed it to have been Mr Southey for Johny Ballantyne told me so and swore to it. But if the feather suits your cap you are perfectly welcome to it."

"Very well Hogg" said he "that is spoken like a man and like yourself. I am satisfied. I thought it was meant as personal to me in particular. But never mind. We are friends again as usual. Sit down and we will go to our breakfast together immediately and it shall never more be mentioned between us."

Mr Southey long afterwards told me that he was not the author of that article and that he believed it to have been written by Scott. If it was it was rather too bad of him but he never said it was not his. It was a review of modern literature in the Edin^r Annual Register. As some readers of these anecdotes may be curious to see the offensive passage in *the Spy* I shall here extract it that work being long ago extinct and only occassionally mentioned by myself as a parent will sometimes mention the name of a dear unfortunate lost child who has been forgotten by all the world beside.

"The papers which have given the greatest personal offence are those of Mr Shuffleton which popular clamour obliged the editor reluctantly to discontinue. Of all the poets and poetesses whose works are there emblematically introduced one gentleman alone stood the test and his firmness was even by himself attributed to foregiveness. All the rest male and female tossed up their noses and pronounced the writer an ignorant and incorrible [sic] barbarian. *The Spy* hereby acknowledges himself the author of these papers and adheres to the figurative characters he has there given of the poetical works of those authors. He knows that in a future edition it is expected that they are all to be altered or obliterated—They never shall! Though the intreaties of respected friends prevailed on him to relinquish a topic which was his favoutite one what he has published he has published and no private consideration shall induce him to an act of such manifest servility as that of making a renounciation. Those who are so grossly ignorant as to suppose the figurative characteristics of the poetry as having the smallest reference to the personal characters of the authors are below reasoning with. And since it has of late become fashionable with some great poets to give an estimate of their great powers in periodical works of distinction surely others have an equal right to give likewise their estimates of the works of such bards. It is truly amusing to see how artfully a gentleman [is placed] at the head of a school of poetry and one who is perhaps his superior at the tail of it. How he can make himself to appear as the greatest genius that ever existed. With what address he can paint his failings as beauties and depict his greatest excellencies as slight defects finding fault only with those parts which every one must admire. The design is certainly an original though not a very creditable one. Great authors cannot remain always concealed let them be as cautious as they will the smallest incident often assisting curiosity in the discovery." *Spy for August 24th* 1811.[13]

This last sentence supposing Sir Walter to have been the author

---

[13] This issue of *The Spy* was in fact the last, and it contains a survey by Hogg of his experiences and activities as editor of the periodical, from which the passage quoted here is taken. "Mr Shuffleton", who makes a number of appearances in early numbers of *The Spy*, operates a large magic mirror, in which he conjures up the muses of the Scottish poets. "He makes these ladies to appear in their common wearing apparel, and walk about, and sing as long as we please: and what is more curious still, if any of us choose to ask a question or two, or make any remarks, they will answer us."

The article in the *Edinburgh Annual Register* to which Hogg refers appears in vol. 1 pt. 2, p. 417–43. This volume relates to 1808, but was published in 1810. The article is a review of "the living poets of Great Britain", and the writer declares: "We do not hesitate to distinguish, as the three most successful candidates for poetical fame, Scott, Southey, and Campbell." Hogg is mentioned as an example of "the poets who daily spring up among the lees of the people and find admirers to patronise them because they write 'wonderfully well *considering.*' This is abstractedly one of the most absurd claims to distinction possible. We do not suppose any living poet, Southey for instance, or Campbell, would gain much credit for making a pair of shoes, although they might be very well made considering. . . .

"The success of Burns had the effect of exciting general emulation among all of his class in Scotland who were able to tag a rhyme. The quantity of Scottish verses with which we were inundated was absolutely overwhelming. Poets began to chirp in every

which I now suspect he was certainly contained rather too broad and too insolent a charge to be passed over with impunity. When I wrote it I believed he was but had I continued to believe so I would not have called on him the next morning after the publication of the paper. Luckily before putting the paper to press I waited on Mr John Ballantyne and asked him who was the author of that insolent paper in his annual Register which placed me as the dregs of all the poets in Britain.

"O the paper was sent to our office by Southey" said he "You know [he] is editor and part proprietor of the work and we never think of objecting to any thing that he sends us. Neither my brother James nor I ever read the article until it was published and we both thought it a good one."

Now this was a story beside the truth for I found out afterwards that Mr James Ballantyne had read the paper from M.S. in a literary long before its publication where it was applauded in the highest terms. I however implicitly believed it as I have done every body all my life. At that period the whole of the aristocracy and literature of our country were set against me and determined to keep me down[14] nay to crush me to a nonentity; thanks be to God I have lived to see the sentiments of my countrymen completely changed.

There was once more and only once that I found Sir Walter in the same querulous humour with me. It was the day after the publication of my *Brownie of Bodsbeck*. I called on him after his return from the parliament House on pretence of asking his advice about some very important advice [sic] but in fact to hear his senti-

corner like grass-hoppers in a sunshine day. The steep rocks poured down poetical goatherds, and the bowels of the earth vomited forth rhyming colliers; but of all the herd we can only distinguish James Hogg, a Selkirkshire shepherd, as having at all merited the public attention; and there cleaves to his poetry a vulgarity of conception and expression which we greatly question his ever being able to overcome. . . .

"The van and rear of the class of occasional poets being thus reviewed, we turn our attention to the main body."

Hogg's quotation from *The Spy* includes the words "and one who is perhaps his superior at the tail of it". These words do not appear in the original passage in *The Spy*, and were no doubt added as a convenient way of explaining some of the allusions in the conversation with Scott which Hogg records. Hogg also makes a number of stylistic changes, but these do not alter the meaning of the passage. In a recent letter to me Dr J. C. Corson points out that Sir Herbert Grierson stated that the article in the *Edinburgh Annual Register* was by Scott (Scott, *Letters* (1932), vol. 2, p. 283); Dr Corson believes this attribution to be correct, although the evidence is not absolutely conclusive. Southey edited the *Register* from 1809 till 1815.

14 "What a horrible conspiracy!"—*Domestic Manners*.

ments of my new work. His shaggy eyebrows were hanging very sore down, a bad prelude, which I knew too well.

"I have read through your new work Mr Hogg" said he and must tell you downright and plainly as I always do that I like it very ill—very ill indeed."

"What for Mr Scott?"

"Because it is a false and unfair picture of the times and the existing characters altogether. An exhaggerated and unfair picture!"

"I dinna ken Mr Scott. It is the picture I hae been bred up in the belief o' sin' ever I was born and I had it frae them whom I was most bound to honour and believe. An' mair nor that there is not one single incident in the tale—not one—which I cannot prove from history to be literally and positively true. I was obliged sometimes to change the situations to make one part coalesce with another but in no one instance have I related a story of a cruelty or a murder which is not literally true. An' that's a great deal mair than you can say for your tale o' Auld Mortality."

You are overshooting the mark now Mr Hogg. I wish it were my tale. But it is *not* with regard to that, that I find fault with your tale at all but merely because it is an unfair and partial picture of the age in which it is laid.

Na, I shouldna hae said it was *your* tale for ye hae said to your best friends that it was not an' there I was wrang. Ye may hinder a man to speak but ye canna hinder him to think an' I can speak at the[15] thinking. But whoever wrote Auld Mortality kenning what I ken an' what ye ken I wadna wonder at you being ill-pleased with my tale if ye thought it written as a counterpoise to that but ye ken weel it was written lang afore the other was heard of.

Yes I know that a part of it was in M.S. last year but I suspect it has been greatly exhaggerated since.

As I am an honest man sir there has not been a line altered or added that I remember of.[16] The original copy was printed. Mr Blackwood was the only man beside yourself who saw it. He read it painfully which I now know you did not and I appeal to him.

Well well. As to its running counter to Old Mortality I have nothing to say. Nothing in the world. I only tell you that with the

---

[15] Hogg's manuscript has "the the".

[16] Although it seems probable that the bulk of *The Brownie* was written before *Old Mortality*, it was not completed until after the publication of Scott's novel. See *Memoir*, p. 44–6.

exception of Old Nanny the crop-eared Covenanter who is by far the best character you ever drew in your life I dislike the tale exceedingly and assure you it is a distorted a prejudiced and untrue picture of the Royal party.

It is a devilish deal truer than your's though; and on that ground I make my appeal to my country." And with that I rose and was going off in a great huff.

"No no! stop" cried he "You are not to go and leave me again[17] in bad humour. You ought not to be offended at me for telling you my mind freely.

Why to be sure it is the greatest folly in the world for me to be sac. But ane's beuks are like his bairns he disna like to hear them spoken ill o' especially when he is concious that they dinna deserve it.

Sir Walter then after his customary short good humoured laugh repeated a proverb about the Gordons which was exceedingly *apropos* to my feelings at the time but all that I can do I cannot remember it though I generally remembered every[thing] that he said of any import. He then added "I wish you to take your dinner with me to day. There will be no body with us but James Ballantyne who will read you something new and I wanted to ask you particularly about something which has escaped me at this moment. Ay it was this. Pray had you any tradition on which you founded that ridiculous story about the Hunt of Eildon."[18]

"Yes I had" said I "as far as the two white hounds are concerned and of the one pulling the poisoned cup twice out of the Kings hand when it was at his lips.

That is very extraordinary" said he "for the very first time I read it it struck me I had heard something of the same nature before but how or where I cannot comprehend. I think it must have been when I was on the nurse's knee or lying in the cradle yet I was sure I had heard it. It is a very ridiculous story that Mr Hogg. The most ridiculous of any modern story I ever read. What a pity it is that you are not master of your own capabilities for that tale might have been made a good one."

[17] Maginn points out that Scott's implied reference here to the quarrel over *The Spy* seems unlikely: "Who fancies that Sir Walter, tenacious as his memory was, remembered any thing of the trumpery publication seven years after it was defunct?" No doubt the "again" is an addition of Hogg's, stemming from the fact that the two quarrels are linked in his narrative, rather than a word actually uttered by Scott.

[18] Published with *The Brownie of Bodsbeck*.

It was always the same on the publication of any of my prose works. When The Three perils of Man appeared he read me a long lecture on my extravagance in demonology and assured me I had ruined one of the best tales in the world. It is manifest however that the tale had made no ordinary impression on him as he subsequently copied the whole of the main plot into his tale of Castle Dangerous.[19]

Sir Walter's conversation was always amusing always interesting. There was a conciseness a candour and judiciousness in it which never was equalled. His anecdotes were without end and I am almost certain they were all made off hand for I never heard one of them either before or after. His were no Joe Miller jokes.[20] The only time ever his conversation was to me perfectly uninteresting was with Mr John Murray of Albemarl street London. Their whole conversation was about noblemen parliamenters and literary men of all grades none of which I had ever heard of or cared about, but every one of which Mr Murray seemed to know with all their characters society and propensities—This information Sir Walter seemed to drink in with as much zest as I did his whisky toddy and this conversation was carried on for two days and two nights with the exception of a few sleeping hours and there I sat beside them all the while like a perfect stump; a sheep who never got in a word not even a bleat. I wish I had the same opportunity again.

I first met with Sir Walter at my own cottage in the wilds of Ettrick forest as above narrated and I then spent two days and two nights in his company. When we parted he shook my hand most heartily and invited me to his cottage on the banks of the North Esk

[19] The "main plot" of the Three Perils concerns a siege of the castle of Roxburgh in the time of Robert II. Sir Philip Musgrave, commander of the English garrison, will win the hand and fortune of the Lady Jane Howard if he holds the castle till Christmas. King Robert offers the hand of his daughter Margaret to the Scottish knight who takes the castle before that time. This is attempted by James Earl of Douglas, and both the Princess and Lady Jane travel to the siege in disguise. Lady Jane is captured by Douglas, who offers her in exchange for the castle. Musgrave kills himself. Douglas, with the somewhat self-seeking help of Sir Ringan Redhough, eventually captures the castle and wins Margaret's hand. Lady Jane marries Sir Charles Scott, a kinsman of Redhough.

In Castle Dangerous, Scott's last published novel, the Lady Augusta of Berkeley offers her hand and fortune to the English knight who can hold Douglas Castle against the Scots for a year and a day, a feat which is attempted by Sir John de Walton. Sir James Douglas sets out to win back his castle from the English invaders, and Lady Augusta travels to the siege in disguise. She is captured by Douglas, who offers her in exchange for the castle. The Scots then win a military advantage over the English, who surrender the castle. Douglas magnanimously allows Sir John and Lady Augusta to return to England in safety.

[20] Joe Miller's Jests was a jest-book by John Mottley, first published in 1739.

above Lasswade. "By all means come and see me" said he "and I will there introduce you to my wife. She is a foreigner. As dark as a blackberry and does not speak the broad Scots so well as you and me. Of course I don't expect you to admire her much but I shall assure you of a hearty welcome.

I went and visited him the first time I had occassion to be in Edin^r expecting to see Mrs Scott a kind of half blackamore whom our sherrif had married for a great deal of money. I knew nothing about her and had never heard of her save from his own description, but the words "as dark as a blackberry" had fixed her colour indelibly on my mind. Judge of my astonishment when I was introduced to one of the most beautiful and handsome creatures as Mrs Scott whom I had ever seen in my life. A brunnette certainly with raven hair and large black eyes but in my estimation a perfect beauty. I found her quite affable and she spoke English very well save that she put always the *d* for the th and left the aspiration of the h out altogether. She called me all her life Mr Og. I understood perfectly well what she said but for many years I could not make her understand what I said. She had frequently to ask an explanation from her husband. And I must say this of Lady Scott though it was well known how jealous she was of the rank of Sir Walter's visitors yet I was all my life received with the same kindness as if I had been a relation or one of the family although one of the most homely of his daily associates! But there were many others both poets and play-actors whom she received with no very pleasant countenance. Jeffery and his sattelites she could not endure and there was none whom she disliked more than Brougham[21] for what reason I do not know but I have heard her misca' him terribly as well as "dat body Jeffery". It might be owing to some reviews which I did not know about. After the review of Marmion appeared she never would speak to Jeffery again for though not a lady who possessed great depth of penetration she knew how to appreciate the great powers of her lord from the beginning and despised all those who ventured to depreciate them.

I have heard Sir Walter tell an anecdote of this review of Marmion.[22] As he and Jeffery Southey Curwin and some other body I

[21] Henry Peter Brougham (1778–1868) was associated with Jeffrey in the establishing of the *Edinburgh Review*.

[22] "We have heard this story with a variation. Jeffrey, in his review of Marmion, while praising the author's talents highly, introduced some censure. Going to sup with

have forgot who were sailing on Derwent Water at Keswick in Cumberland one fine day Mr Jeffery to amuse the party took from his pocket the M.S. of the Review of Marmion and read it throughout. This I think was honest in Jeffery but the rest of the company were astonished at his insolence and at some passages did not know where to look. When he had finished he said "Well Scott! What think you of it? What shall be done about it?"

"At all events I have taken *my* resolution what to do" said Scott "I'll just sink the boat." The Review was a little modified after that.

But to return to lady Scott she is cradled in my remembrance and ever shall as a sweet kind and affectionate creature. When any of the cottagers or retainers about Abbotsford grew ill they durst not tell her as it generally made her worse than the sufferers and I have heard of her groaning and occassionally weeping for a whole day and a good part of the night for an old tailor who was dying and leaving a small helpless family[23] behind him. Her daughter Anne is very like her in the contour and expression of her countenance.

Who was lady Scott originally? I really wish any body would tell me for surely somebody must know. There is a veil of mystery hung over that dear lady's birth and parentage which I have been unable to see through or lift up; and there have been more lies told to me about it and even published in all the papers of Britain by those who *ought* to have known than ever was told about those of any woman that ever was born. I have however a few cogent reasons for believing that the present Sir Walter's grandfather was a nobleman of very high rank.[24]

Scott, he, in the honesty of his heart, took the proof-sheets of the review with him and read them aloud. Mr Jeffrey's manner is unfortunate, and he was considerably Scott's junior. Scott and all his friends (his wife in particular,) took the matter in high dudgeon. The review was not modified."—*Domestic Manners*. Jeffrey in fact sent proofs of the review of *Marmion* to Scott. Later, over dinner, Scott received Jeffrey cordially, but Mrs Scott's resentment was not completely concealed (cf. Edgar Johnson, *Sir Walter Scott* (1970), p. 281–3). It is of course possible that Hogg heard Scott tell the anecdote in the form given in the text.

[23] The word "family" appears twice in Hogg's manuscript.

[24] "This impression, strange to say, was encouraged by Sir Walter. Falconbridge was contented to be a king's bastard. The anxiety to be connected with nobility by a wife's illegitimacy, is a step beyond this, in aristocratical devotion."—*Domestic Manners*. Hogg has sometimes been blamed for this footnote, but if the *Domestic Manners* was indeed a pirated edition, then the footnotes were in no way connected with Hogg. Mrs Scott was the daughter of Jean François Charpentier of Lyons; she became the ward of the Marquis of Downshire, and it was rumoured that she was in fact the illegitimate child of the Marquis. This rumour was incorrect, but Edgar Johnson in discussing this

Like other young authors Sir Walter was rather vain of his early productions and liked to make them the subject of conversation. He recited Glen-Finlas one day to me on horseback long before its publication. He read me also the Lay of the Last Minstrel from M.S. at least he and William Erskine (lord Kineder) and James Ballantyne read it Canto about. He always preferred their readings to his own. Not so with me. I could always take both the poetry and the story along with me better from his reading than any other body's whatsoever. Even with his deep-toned bass voice and his Berwick burr he was a far better reader than he was sensible of.[25] Every thing that he read was like his discourse it always made an impression.

He likewise read me Marmion before it was published but I think it was then in the press for part of it at least was read from proof slips and sheets with corrections on the margin. The Marmion M.S. was a great curiosity. I wonder what became of it. It was all written off hand in post letters from Ashiesteel, Mainsforth, Rokeby and London.

The readings of Marmion began on his own part. I had newly gone to Edin[r] and knew nothing about the work—had never heard of it. But the next morning after my arrival on going to breakfast with him he sought out a proof sheet and read me his description of my beloved St Mary's Lake in one of his introductions I think to canto second to ask my opinion as he said of its correctness as he had never seen the scene but once. I said there never was any thing more graphic written in this world and I still adhere to the assertion so it was no flattery; and I being perfectly mad about poetry then begged of him to let me hear the canto that followed that vivid description expecting to hear something more about my native mountains. He was then to humour me obliged to begin at the beginning of the poem and that day he read me the two first books.

That night my friends Grieve and Morison who were as great enthusiasts as myself expressed themselves so bitterly at my advantage over them that the next morning I took them both with me and they heard him read the two middle cantos which I am sure neither of them will ever forget. When we came to the door Morison said "For God's sake Hogg don't ring."

question writes: "Mysteries, however, in Charlotte's family background there were. . . . Indeed, some of the veils shrouding her origins are still unresolved." (See *Sir Walter Scott* (1970), p. 138 ff.)

[25] "Just."—*Domestic Manners.*

I

"What for?" said I.

"Because I know there will be something so terribly gruff about him I dare not for my soul go in" said he.

"You never were so far mistaken in your life" said I "Sir Walter's manner is just kindness personified" and rung the bell.

When the Lady of the lake was mostly or at least partly in M.S. he said to me one evening "I am going to adventure a poem on the public quite different from my two last perfectly different in its theme stile and measure" on which he took the M.S. from his desk and read me the course of The Fiery Cross and The Battle of the Trossachs. I said "I could not perceive any difference at all between the stile of that and his former poems, save that because it was quite new to me I thought it rather better." He was not quite well pleased with the remark and was just saying I would think differently when I had time to peruse the whole poem when Sir John Hope came in and I heard no more.

After that he never read any thing more to me before publishing save one ghost story. His fame became so firmly established that he cared not a fig for the opinions of his literary friends before hand. But there was one forenoon he said to me in his study I have never durst venture upon a real ghost story Mr Hogg but you have published some such thrilling ones of late[26] that I have been this very day employed in writing one. I assure you "it's no little that gars auld Donald pegh" but yon Lewis stories of your's frightened me so much that I could not sleep and now I have been trying my hand on one and here it is. He read it; but it did not make a great impression on me for I do not know at this moment not having his works by me where it is published. It was about the ghost of a lady and I think appeared in the Abbot or Monastry.[27] He read me also a humorous poem in M.S. which has never been published that I know of. It was something about finding out the happiest man and making him a present of a new holland shirt.[28] Paddy got it who had never known the good of a shirt. Mr Scott asked me what I

[26] In *Winter Evening Tales*, published in 1820 in two volumes by Oliver and Boyd.

[27] The ghostly White Lady of Avenel appears in *The Monastery* (1820).

[28] "It appeared in the 'Sale Room,' a four-penny literary weekly, published by John Ballantyne. It is a circumstance not generally known, that a communication to this publication signed Christopher Corduroy, was the first thing that attracted Scott's notice to Lockhart, of whom he previously knew nothing."—*Domestic Manners*. The poem was "The Search after Happiness; or the Quest of Sultaun Solimaun" (1817).

thought of it. I said the characters of the various nations were exquisitely hit off but I thought the winding up was not so effective as it might have been made. He said he believed I was perfectly right. I never heard what became of that poem or whether it was ever published or not for living in the wilderness as I have done for the last twenty years I know very little of what is going on in the literary world. One of Sir Walter's representatives has taken it upon him to assert that Sir Walter always held me in the lowest contempt! He never was farther wrong in his life but Sir Walter would still have been farther wrong if he had done so. Of that posterity will judge; but I assure that individual that there never was a gentleman in the world who paid more respect or attention to a friend than Sir Walter did to me for the space of the thirty years that we were acquainted. True he sometimes found fault with me but in that there was more kindness than all the rest.

I must confess that before people of high rank he did not much encourage my speeches and stories. He did not hang down his brows then as when he was ill pleased with me but he raised them up and glowred and put his upper lip far over the under one seeming to be always terrified at what was to come out next and then he generally cut me short by some droll anecdote to the same purport of what I was saying. In this he did not give me fair justice for in my own broad homely way I am a very good speaker and teller of a story too.

Mrs Hogg was a favourite of his. He paid always the greatest deference and attention to her. When we were married I of course took her down to Abbotsford and introduced her and though the company was numerous he did her the honour of leading her into the dining-room and placing her by his side. When the ladies retired, he before all our mutual friends present testified himself highly pleased with my choice and added that he wondered how I had the good sense and prudence to make such a one "I dinna thank ye ata' for the compliment Sir Walter" said I.

As for her poor woman she perfectly adored him. There was one day when he was dining with us at Mount Benger on going away he snatched up my little daughter Margaret Laidlaw and kissed her and then laying his hand on her head said "God Almighty bless you my dear child!" on which my wife burst into tears. On my coming back from seeing him into the carriage that stood at the base of the hill I said "What ailed you Margaret."

"O" said she "I thought if he had but just done the same to them all I do not know what in the world I would not have given!"

There was another year previous to that when he was dining with me at the same place he took a great deal of notice of my only son James trying to find out what was in him by a number of simple questions not one of which James would answer. He then asked me anent the boy's capabilities. I said he was a very amiable and affectionate boy but I was afraid he would never be the Cooper of Fogo for he seemed to be blest with a very thick head. "Why but Mr Hogg you know it is not fair to lay the saddle upon a foal" said he "I for my part never liked precocity of genius all my life and can venture to predict that James will yet turn out an honour to you and all your kin." I was gratified by the prediction and lost not a word of it.

The boy had at that time taken a particular passion for knives particularly for large ones and to amuse him Sir Walter showed him a very large gardener's knife which he had in his pocket which contained a saw but I never regarded it and would not have known it the next day. James However never forgot it and never has to this day and I should like very well if that knife is still to be found that James should have it as a keepsake of his father's warmest and most esteemed friend. Col. Ferguson perceiving the boy's ruling passion made him a present of a handsome two bladed knife. But that made no impression on James. Col. Ferguson he forgot the next day but Sir Walter he never forgot till he came back again always denominating him "The man wi' the gude knife."

The last time Margt saw him was at his own house in Maitland-street[29] a very short time before he finally left it. We were passing from Charlotte Square to make a call in Lawrieston when I said "see yon is Sir Walter's house at yon red lamp." "O let me go in and see him once more! said she.

"No no Margt" said I "you know how little time we have and it would be too bad to intrude on his hours of quiet and study at this time of the day. "O but I must go in!" said she "and get a shake of his kind honest hand once more. I cannot go bye." So I knowing that

[29] After his financial ruin Scott gave up his house in Castle Street, and took Edinburgh lodgings first in North St David's Street, then in Walker Street. Hogg appears to have the Walker Street lodgings in mind; West Maitland Street and Walker Street both open into Coates Crescent.

"Nought's to be won at woman's hand
Unless ye gie her a' the plea"

Was obliged to comply. So in we went and were received with all the
affection of old friends but his whole discourse was addressed to my
wife while I was left to shift for myself among books and newspapers.
He talked to her of our family and of our prospects of being able to
give them a good education which he reccommended at every risk
and at every sacrifice. He talked to her of his own family one by one
and of Mr Lockhart's family, giving her a melancholly account of
little Hugh John Lockhart (now the celebrated Hugh Little-John)
who was a great favourite of his but whom as he said that day he
despaired of ever seeing reach manhood.

The only exchange of words I got with him during that short visit
which did not extend to the space of an hour was of a very important
nature indeed. In order to attract his attention from my wife to one
who I thought as well deserved it I went close up to him with a
scrutinizing look and said "Gudeness guide us Sir Walter but ye
hae gotten a braw gown!" On which he laughed and said I got it
made for me in Paris (such a year) when certain great personages
chose to call on me of a morning and I never thought of putting it
on since until the day before yesterday on finding that my every-day
one had been sent to Abbotsford. But I shall always think the more
highly of my braw gown Mr Hogg for your notice of it." I think it
was made of black twilled satin and lined.

But to return to some general anecdotes with which I could fill
volumes. When I first projected my literary paper *the Spy* I went
and consulted him as I generally did in every thing regarding literature. He shook his head and let fall his heavy eye-brows but said
nothing. The upper lip came particularly far down. I did not like
these prognostics at all; so I was obliged to broach the subject again
without having received one word in answer.

"Do you not think it rather dangerous ground to take after Addison Johnson and Henry McKenzie?" said he.

"No a bit!" said I I'm no the least feared for that. My papers may
no be sae yelegant as their's but I expect to make them mair
original."

"Yes they will certainly be original enough with a vengeance"
said he.

I asked him if he thought threepence would be a remunerating price? He answered with very heavy brows that "taking the extent of the sale into proper calculation he suspected she must be a fourpenny cut. He said this it with a sneer which I never could forget. I asked if he would lend me his assistance in it? He said he would first see how I came on and if he saw the least prospect of my success he would support me and with this answer I was obliged to be content. He only sent me one letter for the work inclosing two poems of Leyden's. He was however right in discouraging it and I was wrong in adventuring it.

I never knew him wrong in any of his calculations or inhibitions but once and then I am sure my countrymen will join with me in saying that he was wrong. He wrote me once when I was living in Nithsdale informing me that he was going to purchase the estate of Broadmeadows on Yarrow. That he was the highest offerer and was he believed sure of getting it[30] and that he had offered half and more on my account that I might be his chief Shepherd and manager of all his rural affairs. The plan misgave. Mr Boyd overbid him and became the purchaser on which Sir Walter was so vexed on my account I having kept myself out of a place depending upon his that he actually engaged me to Lord Porchester as his chief Shepherd where I was to have a handsome house a good horse a small pendicle rent free and twenty pounds a year. I approved of the conditions as more than I expected or was entitled to only they were given with this *proviso* that "I was to put my poetical talent under lock and key for ever!" I have the letter. Does any body think Sir Walter was right there? I can't believe it and I am sure my friend the present Lord Porchester would have been the last man to have exacted such a stipulation. I spurned the terms and refused to implement the bargain. This is the circumstance alluded to in the Queen's Wake as a reflection on Walter the Abbot which I think it proper to copy here to save researches for an extract where it may be impossible to find it. It alludes to the magic harp of Ettrick banks and Yarrow Braes.[31]

> "The day arrived blest be the day
> Walter the Abbot came that way
> The sacred relic met his view
> Ah! Well the pledge of heaven he knew!

[30] Hogg's manuscript reads "it it".

[31] See footnote to *Memoir*, p. 66, where "the magic harp" in this passage from *The Queen's Wake* is discussed.

He screwed the chords he tried a strain
'Twas wild—He tuned and tried again
Then poured the numbers bold and free
The ancient magic melody
   The land was charmed to list his lays
It knew the harp of ancient days
The Border Chiefs that long had been
In sepulchres unhearsed and green
Pass'd from their mouldy vaults away
In armour red and stern array
And by their moonlight halls were seen
In vizor helm and habergeon
Even fairies sought our land again
So powerful was the magic strain
   Blest be his generous heart for aye
He told me where the relic lay
Pointed my way with ready will
Afar on Ettrick's wildest hill
Watched my first notes with curious eye
And wonder'd at my minstrelsy
He little weened a parent's tongue
Such strains had o'er my cradle sung
   O could the Bard I loved so long
Reprove my fond aspiring song![32]
Or could his tongue of candour say
That I should throw my harp away?
Just when her notes began with skill
To sound beneath the southern hill
And twine around my bosom's core
How could we part for evermore?
'Twas kindness all. I cannot blame
For bootless is the minstrel flame
But sure a bard might well have known
Another's feelings by his own
            Queen's Wake sixth edition p. 336–7

I never knew any gentleman so shy and chary of his name and interest as Sir Walter was and though I know Allan Cunningham and Captain J. G. Burns[33] will not join me in this "Let every man roose the ford as he finds it" he never would do any thing for me in

---

[32] Hogg's manuscript has "Repprove".

[33] James Glencairn Burns (1794–1865), the son of the poet, who rose to the rank of Colonel in the Indian Army.

that save by the honour of his undeviating friendship and genuine good advices both of which were of great value to me the one insuring me a welcome among all the genteel company of the kingdom and the other tending greatly to guide my path in a sphere with which I was entirely unacquainted and these I set a high value on. But he would never bring me forward in any way by the shortest literary remark in any periodical.[34] Never would review any of my works although he once promised to do it. No he did not promise he only said before several friends to whom he had been speaking very highly of the work that he was thinking of doing it. But seeing I suppose that the poem did not take so well as he had anticipated he never accomplished his kind intent.[35] I asked him the following year why he had not fulfilled his promise to me.

"Why the truth is Hogg" said he "that I began the thing and took a number of notes marking extracts but I found that to give a proper view of your poetical progress and character I was under the necessity of beginning with the ballads and following through *the Wake* and all the rest and upon the whole I felt that we were so much of the same school that if I had said of you as I wished to say I would have been thought by the world to be applauding myself."[36]

I cannot aver that these were Sir Walter's very words but they were precisely to that purport. But I like other disappointed men not being by half quite satisfied with the answer said "Dear Sir Walter ye can never suppose that I belang to your school o' chivalry? Ye are the king o' that school but I'm the king o' the mountain an' fairy school which is a far higher ane nor yours."

[34] Part of a letter from Scott to John Murray reads as follows: "I also send an article on our friend Hogg. It is too long and rather too dogmatical, but if you have room for it it may do our poor friend some good who really requires to have the public attention called to him now and then." (See *Letters*, ed. Grierson, vol. 4 (1933), p. 544.) Grierson adds the following footnote: "This letter to Murray was dated 1818 by my copyist, but I think it must belong to 1815. . . . No review of Hogg was published till his *Poetic Mirror* was reviewed in the July number of 1816. The actual appearance of the early Quarterlies was seldom that of the date the number bore."

The *Poetic Mirror* appeared anonymously in 1816, and the review in the *Quarterly* does not attribute it to Hogg. The anonymous reviewer writes: "The work at present before us is a series of parodies, which want the most essential merits of that species of cheap wit." It is clearly not Scott's article, which does not appear to have been published. Hogg presumably did not know that Scott had sent this article to Murray.

[35] This probably refers to Hogg's long poem, *Queen Hynde*, which was begun and abandoned in 1817, and which Hogg (encouraged by Scott) completed and published in 1825. Cf. *Memoir*, p. 40-1. *Queen Hynde* is one of Hogg's least successful poems.

[36] Hogg's manuscript has no quotes after "myself".

He rather hung down his brows and said "The higher the attempt to ascend the greater might be the fall" and changed the subject by quoting the saying of some old English Baronet in a fox chase.

He paid two high compliments to me without knowing of either and although some other person should have related these rather than me I cannot refrain from it. One of them was derogatory to himself too, a thing which a young poet is not very apt to publsh. He was he said quarter-master to the Edin^r gentlemen cavalry and composed a song for the corps got a friend to learn it and sing it at the Mess but it did not take very well. At length a Mr Robertson got up and said "Come come. That's but a drool of a sang. Let us have Donald M'Donald." On which Donald M'Donald was struck up and was joined in with such glee that all the Mess got up joined hands and danced round the table and added Scott "I joined the ring too and danced as well as I could and there were four chaps all of the Clan Donachie who got soelevated that they got upon the top of the table and danced a highland reel to the song." He did not know it was mine until after he had told the anecdote when I said "Dear man that sang's mine an' was written sax or seven years bygane. I wonder ye didna ken that."

There was another day as we were walking round the north side of St. Andrew's Square to call on Sir C. Sharpe in York Place he said to me laughing very heartily "I found Ballantyne in a fine quandary yesterday as I called on leaving the Parliament House. He was standing behind his desk actually staring and his mouth quite open. I am glad you have come in Mr Scott said he to tell me if you think I am in my right senses to day or that I am in a dream: O it is quite manifest from the question that you are not in your right senses said I. What is the matter? Here is a poem sent me by Mr Gillies to publish in a work of his said he. It is in his own hand writing and the gradation of the ascent is so regular and well managed that I am bound to believe it is his. Well before you came in I read and read on in these two proofs until at last I said to myself Good lord is this the poetry of Mr Gillies that I am reading! I must be asleep and dreaming and then I bit my little finger to prove if I was not asleep and I thought I was not. But sit down and judge for yourself.

"So James read the poem to me from beginning to end" continued he "and[37] then said Now what think you of this. The only thing

---

[37] Hogg's manuscript does not have quotes before "So", after "end" or before "and".

that I can say said I is that the former part of the poem is very like the writing of an eunuch and the latter part like that of a man. The stile is altogether unknown to me but Mr Gillies's it cannot be." I was sorry I durst not inform him it was mine for it had been previously agreed between Mr Gillies and me that no one should know. It was a blank verse poem but I have entirely forgot what it is about. The latter half only was mine.

"So you say that poetry is not the composition of Mr. Gillies?" said James.

"Yes I do positively. The thing is impossible."

"Well sir I can take your word for that; and I have *not* lost my senses nor am I dreaming at all."

There was one day I met with him on the North Bridge on his return from the Court of Session when he took my arm and said "come along with me Hogg I want to introduce you to a real brownie[38] one who does a great deal of work for me for which I am paid rather liberally." I accompanied him in side[?] of the Register Office where a good looking little spruce fellow his deputy clerk I suppose produced papers bunch after bunch to the amount of some hundreds all of which he signed with *W. Scott* laughing and chatting with me all the while.[39] We then took a walk round the Calton Hill till dinner time when I went home with him and met Ballantyne and Terry.[40] I think it was on that day for it was during a walk round the Calton Hill and I never enjoyed that pleasure with him but twice in my life that we were discussing the merits of his several poems. *The lady of [the] lake* had had an unprecedented run previous to that and as it was really my favourite I was extolling it highly assured that I was going on safe ground but I found that he preferred Marmion and said something to the following effect that *the lady of the lake* would always be the favourite with ladies and people who read merely for amusement but that Marmion would have the preference by real judges of poetry. I have heard people of the first discernment express the same opinion since. For me I think in the *lady of the lake* he reached his acme in poetry for in fact the whole both of his poetry and prose have always appeared to me as two splendid arches of which the *lady of the lake* is the keystone of the

[38] A household spirit who performs tasks for farmers.

[39] "We recommend this to the special notice of Mr Wallace of Kelly."—*Domestic Manners.*

[40] Daniel Terry (1780?–1829), actor, playwright and friend of Scott.

one and Guy Mannering and Old Mortality the joint keystones of the other. I should like very well to write a review of his whole works but that lies quite out of my way at present.

The only other walk I ever got with him round and round the Calton hill was several years subsequent to that. At that time I did not believe that he was the author of the celebrated novels for Johny Ballantyne had fairly sworn me out of my original fixed belief so I began about them very freely and he did the same laughing heartily at some of the jokes and often standing still or sitting down and telling me where he thought the author had succeeded best and where least and there were some places where he did not scruple to say he had failed altogether. He never tried to defend any passage when it was attacked but generally laughed at the[41] remarks.

There cannot be a better trait of Sir Walter's character than this. That all who knew him intimately loved him nay many of them almost worshipped him. The affection and subservience of the two Messrs Ballantyne far surpassed description. They were entrusted with all his secrets and all his transactions and faithful to the last and I know that had he taken some most serious advices which James gave him he never would have been involved as he was. In James he always reposed the most implicit confidence. John he likewise trusted with every thing and loved him as a wayward brother but he often broke a joke at his expense. There was one day I was telling the Sherrif some great secret about the author of a certain work or article I have quite forgot what it was when he said "I suspect you are widely misinformed there Mr Hogg for I think I know the author to be a very different person."

"Na na Mr Scott you are clean wrang" said I. "For Johny Ballantyne tauld me an' he coudna but ken."

"Ay but ye should hae ascertained whether it was leeing Johny or true Johny who told you that before you avouched it; for they are two as different persons as exist on the face of the earth" said he. "Had James told you so you might have aver'd it for James never diverges from the right forward truth." As Mr Southey once told me the very same thing I think I am at liberty to publish the sentiments of two such eminent men of the amiable deceased. James was a man of pomp and circumstance but he had a good and affectionate heart. It was too good and too kind for this world and the loss first of his lady and then of his great patron and friend broke it and he

41 Hogg's manuscript reads "the the".

followed him instantly to the land of forgetfulness. How strange it is that all connected with those celebrated Novels have been hunted off the stage of time as it were together! The publisher the author the two printers and last of all the corrector of the press the honest and indefatigable Daniel M'Corkindale. All gone! And none to tell the secrets of that faithful and devoted little community.

There was no man knew Scott so well as James Ballantyne and I certainly never knew a man admire and revere a friend and patron so much. If any person ventured to compare other modern productions with those of Scott he stared with astonishment and took it as a personal insult to himself. There was one time that in my usual rash forward way I said that Miss Ferrier's novels were better than Sir Walter's. James drew himself up. I wish any reader of this had seen his looks of utter astonishment for he was always a sort of actor James. "What do I hear? What do I hear?" cried he with prodigious emphasis "Is it possible sir that I hear such a sentiment drop from *your* lips?" I was obliged to burst out a laughing and run away.

Sir Walter's attached and devoted friends were without number but William Erskine[42] and James Ballantyne were his constant and daily associates. It is a pity that Ballantyne had not left a written character of him for he could and would have done him justice. But the interesting part of their correspondence will soon all come to light in Lockhart's life of his illustrious father-in-law. He was the only man I ever knew whom no man either poor or rich held at ill will. I was the only exception myself that ever came to my knowledge but that was only for a short season and all the while it never lessened his interest in my welfare. I found that he went uniformly on one system. If he could do good to any man he would do it but he would do harm to no man. He never resented a literary attack however virulent of which there were some at first but always laughed at them. This showed a superiority of mind and greatness of soul which no other young author is capable of. He never retaliated but trusted to his genius to overcome all and it was not on a bruised reed that he leaned.

Although so shy of his name and literary assistance which indeed he would not grant to any one on any account save to Lockhart yet to poor men of literary merit his purse strings were always open as far as it was in his power to assist them. I actually knew several un-

[42] William Erskine, Lord Kinneder (1769–1822), advocate and life-long friend of Scott.

successful authors who for years depended on his bounty for their daily bread. And then there was a delicacy in his way of doing it which was quite admirable. He gave them some old papers or old ballads to copy for him pretending to be greatly interested in them for which he sent them a supply every week making them believe that they were reaping the genuine fruit of their own labours.

There was one day when I was chatting with Ballantyne in his office where I was generally a daily visitor as well as my illustrious friend I chanced to say that I never in my life knew a man like Scott for that I knew to a certainty he was at that time feeling himself a successful author lending pecuniary assistance to very many un-successful ones and the best thing of all he never let his left hand know what his right hand was doing.

Ballantyne's face glowed with delight and the tear stood in his eye "You never were more right in your life" said he "You never were more right in your life! And I am glad that you know and so duly appreciate the merits of our noble our invaluable friend. Look here." And with that he turned up his day book and added "some word it seems had reached Scott that Matturin[43] the Irish poet was lying in prison for a small debt and here have I by Mr Scott's orders been obliged to transmit him a bill of exchange for £60s and Matturin is never to know from whom or whence it came." I have said it oft and now say it again for the last time that those who knew Scott only from the few hundreds or I might say hundreds of thousands of volumes to which he has given birth and circulation through the world knew only one half of the man and that not the best half neither. As a friend he was sometimes stern but always candid and sincere and I always found his counsels of the highest value if I could have followed them. I was indebted to him for the most happy and splendid piece of humorous ballad poetry which I ever wrote. He said to me one day after dinner "It was but very lately Mr Hogg that I was drawn by our friend Kirkpatrick Sharpe to note the merits of your ballad The Witch of Fife. There never was such a thing written for genuine and ludicrous humour but why in the name of wonder did you suffer the gude auld man to be burnt skin and bone by the English at Carlisle (for in the first and second editions that was the issue) I never saw a piece of such bad taste in all my life. What had the poor old carl done to deserve such a fate? Only taken a drappy o' drink too much at another man's expense

[43] Charles Robert Maturin (1782–1824), author of *Melmoth the Wanderer*.

which you and I have done often. It is a *finale* which I cannot bear and you *must* bring of[f] the old man by some means or other no matter how extravagant or ridiculous in such a ballad as yon but by all means bring off the fine old fellow for the present termination of the ballad is one which I cannot brook." I went home and certainly brought off the old man with flying colours which is by far the best part of the ballad.[44] I never adopted a suggestion of his either in prose or verse which did not improve the subject. He knew mankind well. He knew the way to the human heart and he certainly had the art of leading the taste of an empire I may say of a world above all men that ever existed. As long as Sir Walter Scott wrote poetry there was neither man nor woman ever thought of either reading or writing any thing but poetry. But the instant that he gave over writing poetry there was neither man nor woman ever read it more! All turned to tales and novels which I among others was reluctantly obliged to do. Yes I was obliged from the tide the irresistible current that followed him to forego the talent which God had given me at my birth and enter into a new sphere with which I had no acquaintance. The world of imagination had been opened wide to me but of the world of real life I knew nothing. Sir Walter knew it in all its shades and gradations and could appreciate any singular character at once. He had a clear head as well as a benevolent heart; was a good man; an anxiously kind husband an indulgent parent and a sincere foregiving friend; a just judge and a punctual correspondent. I believe that he answered every letter sent to him either from rich or poor and generally not very shortly. Such is the man we have lost and such a man we shall never see again. He was truly an extraordinary man; the greatest man in the world. What are kings or Emperors compared with him? Dust and sand! And unless when connected with literary men the greater part of their names either not remembered at all or only remembered with detestation. But here is a name who next to that of William Shakespeare will descend with rapt admiration to all the ages of futurity. And is it not a proud boast for an old shepherd that for thirty years he could call this man friend and associate with him every day and hour that he chose?

Yes it is my proudest boast. Sir Walter sought me out in the wilderness and attached himself to me before I had ever seen him and although I took cross fits with him his interest in me never

[44] "The Witch of Fife" appears in *The Queen's Wake*, and is one of Hogg's most successful poems.

subsided for one day or one moment. He never scrupled to let me know that I behoved to depend entirely on myself for my success in life but at the same time always assured me that I had talents to ensure that success if properly applied and not suffered to run to waste. I was always received in his house like a brother and he visited me on the same familiar footing. I never went into the inner house of Parliament where he sat on which he did not rise and come to me and conduct me to a seat in some corner of the outer house where he would only sit with me two or three minutes. I am sorry to think that any of his relations should entertain an idea that Sir Walter undervalued me for of all men I ever met with not excepting the noblemen and gentlemen in London[45] there never was a gentleman paid more deference to me than Sir Walter and although many of my anecdotes are homely and common place ones I am sure there is not a man in Scotland who appreciates his value more highly or reveres his memory more.

With regard to his family I have not much to say for I know but little. Sophia was a baby when I first visited him about two or three months old and I have watched her progress ever since. By the time she had passed beyond the years of infancy I perceived that she was formed to be the darling of such a father's heart and so it proved. She was a pure child of nature without the smallest particle of sophistication in her whole composition. And then she loved her father so. O how dearly she loved him! I shall never forget the looks of affection that she would throw up to him as he stood leaning on his crutch and hanging over her at the harp as she chaunted to him his favourite old Border Ballads or his own wild highland gatherings. Whenever he came into a room where she was her countenance altered and she often could not refrain from involuntary laughter. She is long ago a wife and mother herself but I am certain she will always cherish the memory of the most affectionate of fathers.

Walter is a fine manly gentlemanly fellow without pride or affectation but without the least spark of his father's genius that I ever could discern and for all the literary company that he mixed with daily in his youth he seemed always to hold literature and poetry in particular in very low estimation. He was terribly cast down at his father's death. I never saw a face of such misery and dejection and though I liked to see it yet I could not help shedding tears on

[45] Hogg refers to his triumphal visit to London in 1832 to arrange for the publication of *Altrive Tales*.

contemplating his features thinking of the jewel that had fallen from his crown.

I always considered Anne as the cleverest of the family; shrewd, sensible, and discerning but I believe a little of a satyrist for I know that when she was a mere girl her associates were terrified for her. Charles is a queer chap and will either make a spoon or spoil a good horn.

Of Lockhart's genius and capabilities Sir Walter always spoke with the greatest enthusiasm more than I thought he deserved for I knew him a great deal better than Sir Walter did[46] and whatever Lockhart may pretend I knew Sir Walter a thousand times better than he did. There is no man now living who knows Scott's character so thoroughly in all its bearings as William Laidlaw does. He was his land steward his amanuensis and managed the whole of his rural concerns and improvements for the period of twenty years and sorry am I that the present Sir Walter did not find it meet to keep Laidlaw on the estate for without him that dear-bought and classical property will be like a carcass without a head.[47] Laidlaw's head made it. He knows the value of every acre of land on it to a tithe and of every tree in the forest with the characters of all the neighbours and retainers. He was[48] to be sure a subordinate but Sir Walter always treated him as a friend inviting Mrs Laidlaw and him down to every party where there was any body he thought Laidlaw would like to meet and Sir Walter called on Mrs Laidlaw once or twice every good day when he was in the country. I have seen him often pop into his breakfast and take his salt herring and tea with us there with as much ease and good humour as if he had come into his brother's house. He once said to me as we were walking out about Abbotslee and I was so much interested in the speech that I am sure I can indite it word by word for Laidlaw was one of my earliest and dearest friends.

"Was it not an extraordinary chance for me that threw Laidlaw into my hands? Without Laidlaw's head I could have done nothing and to him alone I am indebted for all those improvements. I never found a mind so inexhaustible as Laidlaw's. I have met with many

[46] Hogg no doubt refers to his close association with Lockhart in the early days of *Blackwood's Magazine*.

[47] After Scott's death Laidlaw left the Abbotsford estate to become factor to Sir Charles Lockhart Ross, of Balnagowan, in Ross-shire.

[48] Hogg's manuscript has "was was".

of the greatest men of our country but uniformly found that after
sounding them on one or two subjects there their information terminated. But with the worst of all manners of expression Laidlaw's
mind is inexhaustible. Its resources seem to be without end. Every
day every hour he has something new either of theory or experiment
and he sometimes abuses me like a tinker because I refuse to follow
up his insinuations.

Another day he said to me "You know I reccommend[ed] your
friend Laidlaw last year to Lord Mansfield as his factor but was
obliged to withdraw my reccommendation and give his lordship a
hint to relinquish his choice. For in the first place I was afraid that
Laidlaw's precarious health might unfit him for such a responsible
situation and more than that I found that I could not live without
him and was obliged maugre all misfortunes to replace him in his
old situation." I therefore wish from my heart and soul that matters
could have been so arranged that Laidlaw should not have been
separated from Abbotsford for though my own brother has long had
and still has a high responsibility as shepherd and superintendent
of the inclosures I cannot see how the management of the estate can
go on without Laidlaw. Under the law agents it will both cost more
and go to ruin and I say again Without Laidlaw that grand classical
estate is a carcass without a head.

Whenever Sir Walter spoke of any of his two sons which he
frequently did it was always in a jocular way to raise a laugh at their
expense. His description of Walter when he led in Mrs Lockhart a
bride with his false mustachios and whiskers was a source of endless
amusement to him. He was likewise wont often to quote some of
Charles's wise sayings which in the way that he told them never
failed to set the table in a roar of laughter.

Sir Walter had his caprices like other men and when in poor health
was particularly cross but I always found his heart in the right place
and that he had all the native feelings and generosity of a man of
true genius. I am ashamed to confess that his feelings for individual
misfortune were far more intense than my own. There was one day
that I went in to breakfast with him as usual when he said to me with
eyes perfectly staring "Good God Hogg have you heard what has
happened?"

"Na no that I ken o'. What is it that ye allude to Mr Scott?"

"That our poor friend Irving has cut his throat last night or this
morning and is dead."

["] Oo ay! I heard o' that" said I with a coldness that displeased him "But I never heedit it for the truth is that Irving was joost like the Englishman's fiddle the warst faut that he had he was useless. Irving could never have done any good either for himself his family or ony other leevin creature."

I don't know Mr Hogg what that poor fellow might have done with encouragement. This you must at least acknowledge that if he did not write genuine poetry he came the nearest to it of any man that ever failed." These were Sir Walter's very words and I record them in memory of the hapless victim of despair and dissapointed literary ambition. He farther added "For me his melancholly fate has impressed me so deeply and deranged me so much that it will be long before I can attend to any thing again."

He abhorred all sorts of low vices and blackguardism with a perfect detestation. There was one Sunday when he was riding down Yarrow in his carriage attended by several gentlemen on horseback and I being among them went up to the carriage door and he being our sheriff I stated to him with the deepest concern that there was at that moment a cry of *murder* from the Broadmeadows wood and that Will Watherston was murdering Davie Brunton. "Never you regard that Hogg" said he with rather a stern air and without a smile on his countenance. "If Will Watherston murder Davie Brunton and be hanged for the crime it is the best thing that can befal to the parish. Drive on Peter."

He was no great favorer of religion and seldom or never went to church. He was a complete and finished aristocrat and the prosperity of the state was his great concern which prosperity he deemed lost unless both example and precept flowed by regular gradation from the highest to the lowest. He dreaded religion as a machine by which the good government of the country might be deranged if not uprooted. There was one evening when he and Morrit of Rokeby[49] some of the Fergusons and I were sitting over our wine that he said "There is nothing that I dread so much as a very religious woman. She is not only a dangerous person but a perfect shower bath on all

[49] Scott's close friend John Morritt of Rokeby, to whom *Rokeby* was dedicated. In both the New York edition of the *Familiar Anecdotes* and the *Domestic Manners* the name appears as "Marrit". It is sometimes difficult to distinguish between "o" and "a" in Hogg's hand, and although here I have transcribed the manuscript reading as "Morrit", it is impossible to be certain whether the letter in question is "o" or "a". Maginn in his review remarks: "He means Morritt; but the fact is that Hogg scarcely knows the names of Sir Walter's acquaintances."

social conviviality. The enthusiasm of our Scottish ladies has now grown to such a height that I am almost certain it will lead to some dangerous revolution in the state. And then to try to check it would only make the evil worse. If you ever chuse a wife Hogg for God's sake as you value your own happiness don't chuse a *very* religious one."

He had a settled impression on his mind that a revolution was impending over this country even worse than that we have experienced and he was always keeping a sharp look out on the progress of enthusiasm in religion as a dangerous neighbour. There was one day that he and Laidlaw were walking in the garden at Abbotsford during the time that the western portion of the mansionhouse was a builping. The architect's name I think was Mr Paterson.

"Well, do you [know] Laidlaw" said Scott "That I think Paterson one of the best-natured shrewd sensible fellows that I ever met with. I am quite delighted with him for he is a fund of continual amusement to me. If you heard but how I torment him! I attack him every day on the fundamental principles of his own art. I take a position which I know to be false and persist in maintaining it and it [is] truly amazing with what good sense and good nature he supports his principles. I really like Paterson exceedingly."

"O he's verra fine fellow" said Laidlaw "An[50] extrodinar fine fellow an' has a great deal o' comings an' gangings in him. But dinna ye think Mr Scott that it's a great pity he should hae been a preacher?

"A preacher?" said Scott staring at him "Good Lord! what do you mean?"

Aha! It's a' that ye ken about it!" said Laidlaw "I assure you he's a preacher an' a capital preacher too. He's reckoned the best baptist preacher in a' Galashiels an' preaches every Sunday to a great community o' low kind o' fo'ks."

On hearing this Sir Walter (then Mr Scott) wheeled about and halted off with a swiftness Laidlaw had never seen him exercise before exclaiming vehemently to himself "Preaches! G—— d—— him!" From that time forth his delightful colloqueys with Mr Paterson ceased.

There was another time at Abbotsford when some of the Sutherland family (for I dont remember the English title) and many others were there that we were talking of the Earl of Buchan's ornamental improvements at Dryburgh and among other things of the collossal

50 Hogg's manuscript has no quotes before "An".

statue of Wallace which I rather liked and admired but which Sir Walter perfectly abhorred he said these very words. "If I live to see the day when the men of Scotland like the children of Israel shall every one do that which is right in his own eyes *which I am certain either I or my immediate successors will see* I have settled in my own mind long ago what I shall do first. I'll go down and blow up the statue of Wallace with gun powder. Yes I shall blow it up in such stile that there shall not be one fragment of it left! the horrible monster!"

He had a great veneration for the character of Sir William Wallace and I have often heard him eulogize it. He said to me one morning long ago when Miss Porter's work The Scottish Chiefs[51] first appeared "I am grieved about this work of Miss Porter's! I cannot describe to you how much I am dissapointed I wished to think so well of it; and I do think highly of it as a work of genius. But lord help her! Her Wallace is no more our Wallace than Lord Peter is or than King Henry's messenger to Piercy Hotspur. It is not safe meddling with the hero of a country and of all others I cannot endure to see the character of Wallace frittered away to that of a fine gentleman."

Sir Walter was the best formed man I ever saw and laying his weak limb out of the question a perfect model of a man for gigantic strength. The muscles of his arms were prodigious. I remember of one day long ago I think it was at some national dinner in Oman's Hotel that at a certain time of the night a number of the young heros differed prodigiously with regard to their various degrees of muscular strength. A general measurement took place around the shoulders and chest and I as a particular judge in these matters was fixed on as the measurer and umpire. Scott who never threw cold water on any fun submitted to be measured with the rest. He measured most round the chest and to their great chagrin I was next to him and very little short. But when I came to examine the arms! Sir Walter's had double the muscular power of mine and very nearly so of every man's who was there. I declare that from the elbow to the shoulder they felt as if he had the strength of an ox.

There was a gentleman once told me that he walked into Sir Walter's house in Castle street just as the footman was showing another gentleman out and that being an intimate acquaintance he

[51] *The Scottish Chiefs* (1810) was the most notable novel of Jane Porter (1776–1850). It was immensely successful in Scotland, and was translated into German and Russian.

walked straight into Sir Walter's study where he found him stripped with his shirt sleeves rolled up to his shoulders and his face very red. "Good God Scott what is the matter?" said the intruder "Pray may I ask an explanation of this?"

"Why the truth is that I have just been giving your friend Mr Martin a complete drubbing" said Scott laughing "The scoundrel dared me to touch him but with one of my fingers; but if I have not given him a thorough basting he knows himself. He is the most impudent and arrant knave I ever knew. But I think it will be a while before he attempts to impose again upon me." This Mr Martin the gentleman said was some great picture-dealer. But as I never heard Sir Walter mention the feat in his hours of hilarity I am rather disposed to discredit the story. He was always so reasonable and so prudent that I hardly think he would fall on and baste even a knavish picture-dealer black and blue in his own study. The gentleman who told me is alive and well and may answer for himself in this matter.

Sir Walter in his study and in his seat on the Parliament House had rather a dull heavy appearance but in company his countenance was always lighted up and Chauntry[52] has given the likeness of him there precisely. In his family he was kind condescending and attentive but highly imperative. No one of them durst for a moment disobey his orders and if he began to hang down his eyebrows a single hint was enough. In every feature of his face decision was strongly marked. He was exactly what I conceive an old Border Baron to have been with his green jacket his blue bonnet his snow-white locks muscular frame and shaggy eyebrows.

He was said to be a very careless composer yet I have seen a great number of his M.s.s. corrected and enlarged on the white page which he alternatly left a plan which I never tried in my life. He once undertook to correct the press for a work of mine "The Three Perils of women" when I was living in the country and when I gave the M.s. to Ballantyne I said "Now you must send the proofs to Sir Walter he is to correct them for me."

"He correct them for you!" exclaimed Ballantyne "L—d help you and him both! I assure you if he had no body to correct after him there would be a bonny song through the country. He is the most careless and incorrect writer that ever was born of a voluminous and popular writer and as for sending a proof sheet to him we may as

[52] Sir Francis Chantrey's bust is perhaps the best known portrait of Scott.

K

well keep it in the office. He never heeds it. No no you must trust
the correction of the press to my men and me. I shall answer for them
and if I am in a difficulty at any time I'll apply to Lockhart. He is a
very different man and has the best eye for a corrector of any gentleman corrector I ever saw. He often sends me an article written off
hand like your own with[out] the interlineation of a word or the
necessity of correcting one afterwards. But as for Sir Walter he will
never look at either your proofs or his own unless it be for a few
minutes' amusement."[53]

The Whig ascendency in the British cabinet killed Sir Walter.
Yes I say and aver it was that which broke his heart deranged his
whole constitution and murdered him. As I have shown before a
dread of revolution had long preyed on his mind; he withstood it to
the last: he fled from it but it affected his brain and killed him. From
the moment he perceived the veto of a democracy prevailing he lost
all hope of the prosperity and ascendancy of the British empire. He
not only lost hope of the realm but of every individual pertaining to
it as my last anecdote of him will show for though I could multiply
these anecdotes and remarks to volumes yet I must draw them to a
conclusion. They are trivial in the last degree did they not relate to
so great and so good a man. I have depicted him exactly as he was
as he always appeared to me and was reported by others and I revere
his memory as that of an elder brother.

The last time I saw his loved and honoured face was at the little
inn on my own farm in the Autumn of 1830. He sent me word that
he was to pass on such a day on his way from Dumlanrig Castle to
Abbotsford but he was sorry he could not call at Altrive to see Mrs
Hogg and the bairns it being so far off the way. I accordingly waited
at the inn and handed him out of the carriage. His daughter was
with him but we left her at the inn and walked slowly down the way
as far as Mountbenger Burn. He then walked very ill indeed for the
weak limb had become almost completely useless but he leaned on
my shoulder all the way and did me the honour of saying that he
never leaned on a firmer or a surer.[54]

[53] "This must have been 'leein' Johnie.' See *ante* p. 112."—*Domestic Manners*. [In
this edition p. 121.] Hogg's manuscript has no quotes after "amusement".

[54] The letter by Blackwood in which he describes his conversation with Lockhart
about the *Familiar Anecdotes* (see Introduction) contains the following passage: "One
atrocious lie Mr L. was able to detect from his own personal knowledge. Hogg details
to McCrone at great length a melancholy interview he had with Sir Walter on his last
return from Drumlanrig when he says Sir W. called on him with Miss Scott. He makes

We talked of many things past present and to come but both his memory and onward calculation appeared to me then to be considerably decayed. I cannot tell what it was but there was something in his manner that distressed me. He often changed the subject very abruptly and never laughed. He expressed the deepest concern for my welfare and success in life more than I had ever heard him do before and all mixed with sorrow for my worldly misfortunes. There is little doubt that his own were then preying on his vitals. He told me that which I never knew nor suspected before that a certain gamekeeper on whom he bestowed his maledictions without reserve had prejudiced my best friend the young Duke of Buccleuch against me by a story which though he himself knew it to be an invidious and malicious lie yet seeing his Grace so much irritated he durst not open his lips on the subject farther than by saying. "But my lord Duke you must always remember that Hogg is no ordinary man although he may have shot a stray moorcock." And then turning to me he said "Before you had ventured to give any saucy language to a low scoundrel of an English gamekeeper you should have thought of Fielding's tale of Black George."[55]

Sir W. pay him the most extravagant compliments and exalt him far above any poet of the age. And this is all pure fiction, except that Sir W. did call and Mr L. was with him not Miss Scott" (National Library of Scotland MS. 4035, f. 51-4).

The letter's assertion that Hogg makes Scott "pay him the most extravagant compliments and exalt him far above any poet of the age" is scarcely a fair description of what appears in Hogg's surviving manuscript. The letter implies that Hogg was wrong in stating that Scott was accompanied by his daughter, and it also implies that Lockhart was present although Hogg does not mention this. These, however, do not seem to be matters of central importance.

In a letter to Blackwood from Altrive Lake dated 30 September 1830 Hogg appears to refer to this conversation with Scott: "I had a long chat with Sir Walter the day before yesterday here about our proposed publication of my Scottish tales in monthly numbers. He seemed to think a good deal of selection would be required.... But he said ... he should answer for Lockhart's assistance only it was not possible that he could do all and that as little as possible should be left to him ... Sir Walter seems to have grown peculiarly grave of late and completely wants that hilarity of spirits which he used to have. He seems to feel very deeply for the bare state in which I am left with my family and says he is sure I have written plenty that might be made available with proper management" (National Library of Scotland, MS. 4027, f. 194-5).

[55] "And yet Scott could bow down and worship this boy idiot—the plaything of a rascally game keeper—who valued a moorfowl more than a poet—because he was a Duke!"—*Domestic Manners*. Hogg's narrative here has been questioned, on the grounds that it is inconsistent with the known character of Scott and of the Duke. A. L. Strout, however, writes of this passage: "I do not know that the story is fictitious. The following letter sent by William Laidlaw to Scott in March, 1830, would seem to verify it generally" (Strout, "James Hogg's *Familiar Anecdotes of Sir Walter Scott*", *Studies in Philology*, vol. 33 (1936), p. 467-8).

"I never saw that tale" said I "an' dinna ken ought about it. But never trouble your head about that matter Sir Walter for it is awthegither out o' nature for our young chief to entertain ony animosity against me. The thing will never mair be heard of an' the chap that tauld the lees on me will gang to hell that's aye some comfort."

I wanted to make him laugh but I could not even make him smile. "You are still the old man Hogg careless and improvident as ever" said he with a countenance as gruff and demure as could be.

Before we parted I mentioned to him my plan of trusting an edition of my prose tales in twenty volumes to Lockhart's editing. He disapproved of the plan decidedly and said "I would not for any thing in the world that Lockhart should enter on such a responsibility for taking your ram-stam way of writing into account the responsibility would be a very heavy one. Ay and a dangerous one too!" Then turning half round leaning on his crutch and fixing his eyes on the ground for a long space he said "You have written a great deal that might be made available Hogg with proper attention. And I am sure that one day or other it will be made available to you or your family. But in my opinion this is not the proper season. I wish you could drive off the experiment until the affairs of the nation are in better keeping for at present all things and literature in particular are going straight down hill to destruction and ruin." And then he mumbled something to himself which I took to be an inward curse. I say again and I am certain of it that the democratic ascendancy and the grievous and shameful insults he received from the populace of his own country broke the heart and killed the greatest man that ever that country contained.[56]

When I handed him into the coach that day he said something to me which in the confusion of parting I forgot and though I tried to recollect the words the next minute I could not and never could again. It was something to the purport that it was likely it would be long ere [he] leaned as far on my shoulder again but there was an expression in it conveying his affection for me or his interest in me which has escaped my memory for ever.

This is my last anecdote of my most sincere and esteemed friend. After this I never saw him again. I called twice at Abbotsford during

---

[56] "Bravo Hogg."—*Domestic Manners*. At the election of 1831 Scott spoke in Jedburgh in support of the Tory candidate, Henry Scott. Popular demands for Reform were at their height; Scott's carriage was stoned, and there were shouts of "Burke Sir Walter!"

his last ilness but they would not let me see him and I did not at all regret it for he was then reduced to the very lowest state of degradation to which poor prostrate humanity could be subjected. He was described to me by one who saw him often as exactly in the same state with a man mortally drunk who could in nowise own or assist himself the pressure of the abcess on the brain having apparently had the same effect as the fumes of drunkenness. He could at short intervals distinguish individuals and pronounce a few intelligible words but these lucid glimpses were of short duration the sunken eye soon ceased again from distinguishing objects and the powerless tongue became unable to utter a syllable though constantly attempting it which made the sound the most revolting that can be conceived.

I am sure Heaven will bless Lockhart for his attentions to the illustrious sufferer. The toil and watching that he patiently endured one would have thought was beyond human nature to have stood and yet I never saw him look better or healthier all the while. He will not miss his reward. I followed my friend's sacred remains to his last narrow house remained the last man at the grave and even then left it with reluctance

> Omnes eodem cogimur omnium
> Versatur urna serius ocyus
> Sors exitura.[57]

[57] "Saul among the prophets! Hogg quoting Latin!"—*Domestic Manners*. The quotation is from Horace (*Odes*, II, iii). Horace speaks of the dead being collected like a flock of sheep: "We are all being gathered to the same fold; the lot of all of us is tossing about in the urn, destined sooner or later to come forth."

COMMENTARY

AT the end of the first paragraph of Hogg's manuscript of the *Familiar Anecdotes* there appears the instruction to the printer: "then copy the whole of the Reminiscences of him in The Altrive Tales". The version printed in the *Familiar Anecdotes* differs somewhat from the *Altrive Tales* text, however. No doubt some of the changes can be attributed to Bloodgood, but many of them appear to be authorial. Possibly Hogg noted some revisions on a copy of *Altrive Tales*, and enclosed this copy when he sent his manuscript to Bloodgood. This section of the text appears as follows in the *Familiar Anecdotes* (cf. Memoir, p. 61-6):

The first time I ever saw Sir Walter was one fine day in the summer of 1801. I was busily engaged working in the field at Ettrickhouse, when old Wat Shiel came posting over the water to me and told me that I boud to gang away down to the Ramsey-cleuch as fast as my feet could carry me, for there were some gentlemen there who wanted to see me directly.

'Wha can be at the Ramsey-cleuch that want to see me, Wat."

"I coudna say, for it wasna me they spake to i' the bygangin', but I'm thinking it's the SHIRRA an' some o' his gang."

"I [sic] was rejoiced to hear this, for I had seen the first volumes of the "Minstrelsy of the Border," and had copied a number of ballads from my mother's recital, or chaunt rather, and sent them to the editor preparatory to the publication of a third volume. I accordingly flung down my hoe and hasted away home to put on my Sunday clothes, but before reaching it I met the SHIRRA and Mr. William Laidlaw, coming to visit me. They alighted, and remained in our cottage a considerable time, perhaps, nearly two hours, and we were friends on the very first exchange of sentiments. It could not be otherwise, for Scott had no duplicity about him, he always said as he thought. My mother chaunted the ballad of Old Maitlan' to him, with which he was highly delighted, and asked her if she thought it ever had been in print? And her answer was, "O na, na, sir, it never was printed i' the world, for my brothers an' me learned

it an' many mae frae auld Andrew Moor, and he learned it frae auld
Baby Mettlin, wha was housekeeper to the first laird of Tushilaw.
She was said to hae been another nor a gude ane, an' there are many
queer stories about hersel', but O, she had been a grand singer o'
auld songs an' ballads."

"The first laird of Tushilaw, Margaret?" said he, "then that must
be a very old story indeed?"

"Ay, it is that, sir! It is an auld story! But mair nor that, excepting
George Warton an' James Stewart, there war never ane o' my sangs
prentit till ye prentit them yoursel', an' ye hae spoilt them awthegither. They were made for singing an' no for reading; but ye hae
broken the charm now, an' they'll never be sung mair. An' the worst
thing of a', they're nouther right spell'd nor right setten down."

"Take ye that, Mr. Scott," said Laidlaw.

Scott answered with a hearty laugh, and the quotation of a stanza
from Wordsworth, on which my mother gave him a hearty rap on
the knee with her open hand, and said, "Ye'll find, however, that it
is a' true that I'm tellin' ye." My mother has been too true a
prophetess, for from that day to this, these songs, which were the
amusement of every winter evening, have never been sung more.

We were all to dine at Ramsey-cleuch with the Messrs. Brydon,
but Scott and Laidlaw went away to look at some monuments in
Ettrick church-yard, and some other old thing, I have forgot what,
and I was to follow. On going into the stable-yard at Ramsey-cleuch
I met with Mr. Scott's groom, a greater original than his master, at
whom I asked if the SHIRRA was come?

"Oo ay, lad, the Shirra's come," said he. "Are ye the chap that
mak's the auld ballads, an' sings them sae weel?"

I said, I fancied I was he that he meant, though I could not say
that I had ever made ony very auld ballads.

"Ay, then, lad, gang your ways into the house, and speir for the
Shirra. They'll let ye see where he is, an' he'll be very glad to see ye,
that I'll assure ye o'."

During the sociality of the evening, the discourse ran very much
on the different breeds of sheep, that everlasting drawback on the
community of Ettrick Forest. The original black-faced forest breed
being always denominated the *short sheep*, and the Cheviot
breed the *long sheep*. The [sic] disputes at that time ran very high
about the practicable profits of each. Mr. Scott, who had come
into that remote district to visit a bard of Nature's own making

and preserve what little fragments remained of the country's legendary lore, felt himself rather bored with the everlasting question of the long and short sheep. So, at length, putting on his most serious calculating face, he turned to Mr. Walter Brydon, and said, "I am rather at a loss regarding the merits of this *very* important question. How long must a sheep actually measure to come under the denomination of *a long sheep?*"

Mr. Brydon, who, in the simplicity of his heart, neither perceived the quiz nor the reproof, fell to answer with great sincerity, "It's the woo', sir; it's the woo' that mak's the difference, the lang sheep hae the short woo' an' the short sheep hae the lang thing, an' these are just kind o' names we gie them, ye see."

Laidlaw got up a great guffaw, on which Scott could not preserve his face of strict calculation any longer; it went gradually awry, and a hearty laugh followed. When I saw the very same words repeated near the beginning of the Black Dwarf, how could I be mistaken of the author? It is true that Johnie Ballantyne swore me into a nominal acquiescence to the contrary for several years, but in my own mind I could never get the better of that and several other similar coincidences.

The next day we went off, five in number, to visit the wilds of Rankleburn, to see if, on the farms of Buccleuch and Mount Comyn, the original possession of the Scotts, there were any relics of antiquity which could mark out the original residence of the chiefs whose distinction it was to become the proprietors of the greater part of the border districts. We found no remains of either tower or fortalice, save an old chapel and church-yard, and the remnants of a kiln-mill and mill-dam, where corn never grew, but where, as old Satchells very appropriately says:

"Had heather bells been corn o' the best,
The Buccleuch mill would have had a noble grist."

It must have been used for grinding the chief's black mails, which it is well known were all paid to him in kind; and an immense deal of victual is still paid to him in the same way, the origin of which no man knows.

Besides having been mentioned by Satchells, the most fabulous historian that ever wrote, there was a remaining tradition in the country that there was a font-stone of blue marble, out of which the ancient heirs of Buccleuch were baptized, covered up among the ruins of the old church. Mr. Scott was curious to see if we could discover it, but on going among the ruins where the altar was known to have been, we found the rubbish at that spot dug out to the foundation, we knew not by whom, but it was manifest that the font had either been taken away, or that there was none there. I never heard since that it had ever been discovered by any one.

As there appeared, however, to have been a sort of recess in the eastern gable, we fell a turning over some loose stones, to see if the baptismal font was not there, when we came to one-half of a small pot encrusted thick with rust. Mr. Scott's eyes brightened and he swore it was part of an ancient consecrated helmet. Laidlaw, however, fell a picking and scratching with great patience until at last he came to a layer of pitch inside, and then, with a malicious sneer, he said, "The truth is, Mr. Scott, it's nouther mair nor less than an auld tar-pot, that some of the farmers hae been buisting their sheep out o' i' the kirk lang syne." Sir Walter's shaggy eye-brows dipped deep over his eyes, and, suppressing a smile, he turned and strode away as fast as he could, saying, that "we had just rode all the way to see that there was nothing to *be* seen."

He was, at that time, a capital horseman, and was riding on a terribly high-spirited grey nag, which had the perilous fancy of leaping every drain, rivulet, and ditch that came in our way. The consequence was, that he was everlastingly bogging himself, while sometimes the rider kept his seat in spite of the animals' plunging, and at other times he was obliged to extricate himself the best way he could. In coming through a place called the Milsey Bog, I said to him, "Mr. Scott, that's the maddest de'il of a beast I ever saw. Can you no gar him tak' a wee mair time? he's just out o' ae lair intil another wi' ye."

"Ay," said he, "he and I have been very often like the Pechs (*Picts*) these two days past, we could stand straight up and tie the latchets of our shoes." I did not understand the allusion, nor do I yet, but those were his words.

We visited the old castles of Tushilaw and Thirlstane, dined and spent the afternoon and the night with Mr. Brydon of Crosslee. Sir Walter was all the while in the highest good humour, and seemed to enjoy the range of mountain solitude which we traversed, exceedingly. Indeed, I never saw him otherwise in the fields. On the rugged mountains, and even toiling in the Tweed to the waist, I have seen his glee surpass that of all other men. His memory, or, perhaps I should say, his recollection, was so capacious, so sterling, and minute, that a description of what I have witnessed regarding it would not gain credit. When in Edinburgh, and even at Abbotsford, I was often obliged to apply to him for references in my historical tales, that so I might relate nothing of noblemen and gentlemen named that was not strictly true. I never found him at fault. In that great library, he not only went uniformly straight to the book, but ere ever he stirred from the spot, turned up the page which contained the information I wanted. I saw a pleasant instance of this retentiveness of memory recorded lately of him, regarding Campbell's PLEASURES OF HOPE, but I think I can relate a more extraordinary one.

He, and Skene of Rubislaw, and I were out one night about midnight, leistering kippers in Tweed, about the end of January, not long after the opening of the river for fishing, which was then on the tenth, and Scott having a great range of the river himself, we went up to the side of the Rough haugh of Elibank; but when we came to kindle our light, behold our peat was gone out. This was a terrible disappointment, but to think of giving up our sport was out of the question, so we had no other shift save to send Rob Fletcher all the way through the darkness, the distance of two miles, for another fiery peat.

The night was mild, calm, and as dark as pitch, and while Fletcher was absent we three sat down on the brink of the river, on a little green sward which I never will forget, and Scott desired me to sing them my ballad of "Gilman's-cleuch." Now, be it remembered, that this ballad had never been printed, I had merely composed it by rote, and, on finishing it three years before, had sung it once over to Sir Walter. I began it, at his request, but at the eighth or ninth stanza I stuck in it, and could not get on with another verse, on which he began it again and recited it every word from beginning to end. It being a very long ballad, consisting of eighty-eight stanzas, I testified my astonishment, knowing that he had never heard it but once, and even then did not appear to be paying particular attention. He said he had been out with a pleasure party as far as the opening of the Frith of Forth, and, to amuse the company, he had recited both that ballad and one of Southey's, (The Abbot of Aberbrothock,) both of which ballads he had only heard once from their respective authors, and he believed he recited them both without misplacing a word.

Rob Fletcher came at last, and old Mr. Laidlaw of the Peel with him, carrying a lantern, and into the river we plunged in a frail bark which had suffered some deadly damage in bringing up. We had a fine blazing light, and the salmon began to appear in plenty, "turning up sides like swine;" but wo be to us, our boat began instantly to manifest a disposition to sink, and in a few minutes we reached Gleddie's Weal, the deepest pool in all that part of Tweed. When Scott saw the terror that his neighbour old Peel was in, he laughed till the tears blinded his eyes. Always the more mischief the better sport for him. "For God's sake, push her to the side!" roared Peel. "Oh, she goes fine," said Scott.

> " 'An' gin the boat war bottomless,
> An' seven miles to row.' "

A verse of an old song; and during the very time he was reciting these lines, down went the boat to the bottom, plunging us all into Tweed, over head and ears. It was no sport to me, at all, for I had no change of raiment at Ashiesteel, but that was a glorious night for Scott, and the next day was no worse.

I remember leaving my own cottage here one morning with him, accompanied by my dear friend, William Laidlaw, and Sir Adam Ferguson, to visit the tremendous solitudes of Loch-Skene and the Grey-mare's-tail. I conducted them through that wild region by a path, which, if not rode by Clavers, as reported, never was rode by another gentleman. Sir Adam rode inadvertantly into a gulf and got a sad fright, but Sir Walter, in the very worst paths, never dismounted, save at Loch-Skene to take some dinner. We went to Moffat that night, where we met with Lady Scott and Sophia, and such a day and night of glee I never witnessed. Our very perils were to him matter of infinite merriment; and then there was a short tempered boot-boy at the inn, who wanted to pick a quarrel with him for some of his sharp retorts, at which Scott laughed till the water ran over his cheeks.

I was disappointed in never seeing some incident in his subsequent works laid in a scene resembling the rugged solitude around Loch-Skene, for I never saw him survey any with so much attention. A single serious look at a scene generally filled his mind with it, and he seldom took another. But, here, he took the names of all the hills, their altitudes, and relative situations with regard to one another, and made me repeat all these several times. Such a scene may occur in some of his works which I have not seen, and I think it will, for he has rarely ever been known to interest himself either in a scene or a character, which did not appear afterwards in all its most striking peculiarities.

There are not above three people now living, who, I think, knew Sir Walter better and who understood his character better than I did, and I once declared that if I outlived him, I should draw a mental and familiar portrait of him, the likeness of which to the original could not be disputed. In the meantime, this is only a reminiscence, in my own homely way, of an illustrious friend among the mountains. That revered friend is now gone, and the following pages are all that I deem myself at liberty to publish concerning him.

The enthusiasm with which he recited and spoke of our ancient ballads, during that first tour through the Forest, inspired me with a determination immediately to begin and imitate them, which I did, and soon grew tolerably good at it. I dedicated "The Mountain Bard," to him.

> Bless'd be his generous heart, for aye,
> He told me where the relic lay,
> Pointed my way with ready will,
> Afar on Ettrick's wildest hill;
> Watch'd my first notes with curious eye,
> And wonder'd at my minstrelsy:
> He little ween'd a parent's tongue
> Such strains had o'er my cradle sung.

INDEX

Abbot, The (Scott), 112
Abbotsford, 110, 113, 115, 126–7, 129, 134
Aikman, Andrew, 21, 79–80, 85–6
Aitken, Samuel, 28
"All-Hallow Eve" (Hogg), 40
Altrive Lake Farm, 52–4
Altrive Tales (Hogg), 60–1
Anderson, Robert, 60
Anderson, Samuel, 80
Anster Fair (Tennant), 27

Bailey, Nathan, 9
Ballantyne, James, 19, 39, 76, 105, 107, 111, 119, 120–3, 131–2
Ballantyne, John, 47, 63, 76, 78, 103, 105, 121, 138
Black Dwarf (Scott), 63, 138
Black House Farm, 9
Blackwood, William, 15, 28, 30, 37, 41–6, 53, 56–60
Blackwood's Magazine, 41–4, 59, 76–7
Blind Harry, 8
Border Garland (Hogg), 51
Bowhill, 96–100
Bridal of Polmood (Hogg), 45
Brougham, Henry Peter, 109
Brown, David, 19
Browne, James, 85–6
Brownie of Bodsbeck (Hogg), 44–6, 51, 105–7
Bryden, *farmer of Crosslee*, 4–5, 64, 139
Bryden, Walter, *of Ramseycleuch*, 62, 137–8
Buccleuch, Charles, *4th Duke*, 52–3, 96–100
Buccleuch, Harriet, *Duchess*, 52–3
Buccleuch, Walter Francis, *5th Duke*, 133
Buchan, *Earl of*, 129
Burnet, Thomas, 9
Burns, James Glencairn, 117
Burns, Robert, 11–12, 71

Byron, George Gordon, *6th Baron*, 24, 34, 37–9, 90–1

Cadell, Robert, 57–8
Campbell, Thomas, 64, 140
Castle Dangerous (Scott), 108
Chaldee Manuscript (Hogg and others), 43–4
Chantrey, *Sir* Francis Legatt, 131
Chiefswood, 60
Claverhouse, *see* Graham, John (of Claverhouse)
Cleghorn, James, 42–3
"Connel of Dee" (Hogg), 32
Constable, Archibald, 17, 19, 25, 27–8, 33–6, 43, 57–8
Cromek, Robert Hartley, 73
Cunningham, Allan, 55, 71–4, 117
Cunningham, James, 72–3
Cunningham, Thomas Mouncey, 19, 72

De Quincey, Thomas, 70–1
Don, *Sir* Alexander, 99–100
"Donald MacDonald" (Hogg), 14–15, 119
Dramatic Tales (Hogg), 39, 51
Drumlanrig Castle, 132
Dunlop, William, 26

Edinburgh Annual Register, 103–5
Erskine, William 111, 122
Ettrick Hall Farm, 4, 136
Ettrick House Farm, 4–5, 10, 61
Excursion, The (Wordsworth), 68–9, 71

"Fareweell to Ettrick" (Hogg), 16
Ferguson, *Sir* Adam, 65, 96, 141
Ferrier, Susan, 122
"Field of Waterloo" (Hogg), 48
Fielding, Henry, 133
Fisher, John, *Bp. of Salisbury*, 31
Forest Minstrel, The, (Hogg) 19, 51

Forum, The, 23–4

Galt, John, 74–5
Gentle Shepherd (Ramsay), 8
George IV, King, 59–60
Gillies, Robert Pierce, 119–20
"Gilmanscleuch" (Hogg), 64, 140
"Glenfinlas" (Scott), 111
Goldie, George, 25, 27–8, 30, 86–90
Graham, John (of Claverhouse), 65, 141
Gray, James, 22, 24–5
Grieve, John, 12, 22–4, 29, 36, 44, 48, 111
"Gude Greye Katte, The" (Hogg), 39
Guy Mannering (Scott), 121

Hamilton, Thomas, 78
Harkness, *farmer of Mitchell-Slack*, 17, 71
"Haunted Glen, The" (Hogg), 40
Hogg, James: for words by Hogg, *see* under title
Hogg, James, *son*, 114
Hogg, Margaret Laidlaw, *daughter*, 113
Hogg, Margaret Laidlaw, *mother*, 4, 61–2, 136–7
Hogg, Margaret Phillips, *wife*, 53–4, 113–5
Hogg, Robert, *father*, 4, 69
Hogg, William, *brother*, 10, 13
Hope, *Sir* John, 112
Hunt of Eildon, The (Hogg), 45, 107
Hunting of Badlewe, The (Hogg), 30, 40, 50

Isle of Palms (Wilson), 29
Izett, Chalmers, 31–2

Jacobite Relics (Hogg), 49, 51
Jeffrey, Francis, 26–7, 73–4, 109–10
Jerdan, William, 41

Kinnaird House, 31–2

Lady of the Lake (Scott), 112, 120
Laidlaw, *farmer of Black House*, 9–10

Laidlaw, *farmer of Elibank on Tweed*, 8
Laidlaw, *farmer of Willenslee*, 8–9
Laidlaw, Alexander, 13
Laidlaw, Margaret (Hogg's mother), *see* Hogg, Margaret Laidlaw
Laidlaw, William, 12–13, 61, 63, 65, 126–7, 129, 136–7, 141
Lasswade, 109
Lay of the Last Minstrel (Scott), 111
Leyden, John, 116
Life and Adventures of Sir William Wallace (Blind Harry), 8
Lloyd, Charles, 37, 70
Lockhart, Hugh John, 115
Lockhart, John Gibson, 43–4, 60, 75–9, 95, 115, 122, 126, 132, 134–5
Lockhart, Sophia, 125, 127
Longman & Co., Publishers, 41, 53–4, 56–7

M'Corkindale, Daniel, 122
Mador of the Moor (Hogg), 32, 50
Mansfield, *Lord*, 127
Marmion (Scott), 109–11, 120
Maturin, Charles Robert, 123
Midsummer Night Dreams (Hogg), 32
Minstrelsy of the Scottish Border (Scott), 16, 61–2, 136–7
Monastery, The (Scott), 112
Montagu, *Lord* (brother of Charles, Duke of Buccleuch), 53
Morehead, Robert, 29, 37
Morritt, John Bacon Sawney, 128
Mount Benger Farm, 53–4, 113
Mountain Bard, The (Hogg), 3, 17, 51, 66, 142
Murray, John, 30, 36, 53, 108

Nicol, James, 12
Nithsdale, 17, 116
Noctes Ambrosianae, 70, 77, 80, 86

Odontist, 77–8
"Old Maitland", 61–2, 136–7
Old Mortality (Scott), 44–6, 106–7, 121
Oliver & Boyd, Publishers, 14, 50, 53, 89

Park, James, 32, 75
Paterson, Walter, 34, 37
Peel, *Sir* Robert, 60
Phillips, Margaret (Hogg's wife), *see* Hogg, Margaret Phillips
Pilgrims of the Sun (Hogg), 32–7, 39, 50
Poetic Mirror (Hogg), 37–9, 50, 69–70
Porchester, *Lord*, 116
Porter, Jane, 130
Pringle, Thomas, 37, 39, 42
Private Memoirs and Confessions of a Justified Sinner (Hogg), 51, 55–6

Queen Hynde (Hogg), 40–1, 51, 56, 58
Queen's Wake (Hogg), 23–8, 30–1, 41, 50, 66, 116–8
Queer Book (Hogg), 51

Ramsay, Allan, 8
Right and Wrong Club, 46–7
Robertson, James, 20–1
Rogers, Samuel, 37
Royal Jubilee, The (Hogg), 51, 59–60

Sacred Melodies (Hogg), 51
Satchells, *see* Scot, Walter, of Satchells
Scot, Walter, *of Satchells*, 63, 138
Scott family (of Harden), 95–7
Scott, *farmer of Singlee*, 7–8
Scott, Anne, *daughter of Sir Walter*, 126
Scott, Charles, *son of Sir Walter*, 126–7
Scott, Charlotte, *wife of Sir Walter*, 109–10
Scott, Henry, 22–3, 48
Scott, James, 76–8
Scott, John, 11
Scott, Sophia, *daughter of Sir Walter*, *see* Lockhart, Sophia
Scott, *Sir* Walter, 3–4, 16–17, 24–5, 29–30, 34, 38–9, 41, 44–8, 58, 61–6, 73, 77, 90–1, 95–135, 136–42

Scott, Walter, *son of Sir Walter*, 125–7
Scottish Chiefs, The (Porter), 130
Scottish Pastorals (Hogg), 15–16
Sharpe, Charles Kirkpatrick, 30, 123
Shepherd's Calendar, The (Hogg), 51
Shepherd's Guide, The (Hogg), 17
Shuffleton, Mr, 103–4
Siddons, Henry, 24
Sir Anthony Moore (Hogg), 39–40
Songs, 1831 (Hogg), 15, 51
Southey, Robert, 37, 65, 67–8, 103, 105, 109, 121, 140
Spy, The (Hogg), 19–22, 24, 41, 51, 79–80, 102–5, 115–16
Star, The (newspaper), 21, 85
"Superstition" (Hogg), 32
Sym, Robert, 22, 76, 79–81

"Tam o' Shanter" (Burns), 11
Tennant, William, 27
Terry, Daniel, 120
Thomson, George, 44
Three Perils of Man, The (Hogg), 51, 55, 100–2, 108
Three Perils of Woman, The (Hogg), 55, 131

Wallace, *Sir* William, 8–9, 130
"Will an' Keatie" (Hogg), 15, 83
Wilson, James, 68–69
Wilson, John, 29, 37, 43–4, 48–9, 70, 76
Wilson, Robert, 79
Winter Evening Tales (Hogg), 32, 45, 50–1
"Witch of Fife" (Hogg), 39, 123–4
Woolgatherer, The (Hogg), 45
Wordsworth, Dorothy, 69–70
Wordsworth, William, 37–9, 41, 68–71, 137

"Yarrow Unvisited" (Wordsworth), 69
"Yarrow Visited" (Wordsworth), 69